# PLANNING
## your
# FUTURE

. . .

*a guide for*

## PROFESSIONAL
## WOMEN

### Janet L. Skarbek

THE PROFESSIONAL WOMEN'S INSTITUTE

Cinnaminson, New Jersey

Published by The Professional Women's Institute

PO Box 2590

Cinnaminson, NJ 08077

Phone: (856)786-2573

Fax (856)786-1688

See the last page of this book for information about ordering copies of this book or obtaining information about Janet Skarbek's seminars.

Manufactured in the United States of America

Book production by Indypub

Cover design: Rosie Grupp

This book is designed to provide information about the subject matter covered. It is sold with the understanding that the publisher, author, and advisors are not rendering legal, accounting, or other professional services. If legal or other expert assistance is required, the services of a competent professional should be sought. The publisher, author, and advisors assume no responsibility for errors or omissions.

Skarbek, Janet L.
    Planning your future : a guide for professional women
/ written by Janet Skarbek. -- 1st ed.
    p. cm.
    Includes bibliographical references and index.
    LCCN: 00-134096
    ISBN: 0-9702344-7-3

    1. Businesswomen. 2. Career development. 3. Success in business. 4. Women--Employment. I. Title.

HF5382.6.S53 2001          650.1'082
                          QBI00-751

*Dedicated to the unlimited achievements*
*that lie within you.*

# TABLE OF CONTENTS

# PART II: ADDITIONAL THINGS YOU NEED TO KNOW

# Acknowledgments

First and foremost, thanks to my family who is a living example of unconditional love and support. To my husband, who throughout the three years from conception to publication never questioned whether my pursuit was in vain. To my daughter, for the thousands of smiles she has brought to my lips by just being. To my mother, for enduring countless hours brainstorming with me and for being an active participant in bringing this book to life. To my father, brother, and sister, for being there for me for any reason, always. I love you all.

Thank you to all the friends who listened to my ideas and provided feedback on various issues. Special thanks to Denise Skarbek and Barbara Kelley, for providing fresh perspectives.

To Robert Donnell, for being a role model for following one's dreams and bucking the system. To Margaret Lupoli, for being a role model of a strong assertive woman. To Jay Donnell, for being a kind soul. To the Prestons and Peggy Wasiolek, for being such great neighbors and dear friends.

To Willamette Industries, for showing me that good companies can thrive and maximize their bottom line while truly being interested in the well-being of their employees. To Greg Hawley, for being a role model who demonstrates that good family-friendly values can start at the top of a company and be replicated throughout.

To the Birth Center in Bryn Mawr, Pennsylvania where my greatest dream came true with the birth of my daughter, and where an equally great dream will come true in the near future with the birth of my son.

To all the Villanova University alumni women who participated in the study. Thank you for opening up your lives, hearts, and souls to me. Your response and support have been overwhelming. I am indebted to you for the insights you have provided into your personal and professional lives.

# Introduction

When women are *prepared* for what lies ahead in life and *plan* accordingly to meet their goals, they can achieve their highest aspirations. When women are unprepared for what lies ahead, they will not achieve what they otherwise could have. Women often fail to achieve their goals (or lower their expectations) because they are not prepared to face the challenges that are pivotal to their advancement. College prepares women to meet the technical aspects of their careers, but does little to prepare women for real world issues that are just as important.

The first ten to fifteen years following college graduation are the most important in a woman's life for *directing her future.* The decisions made during this period will have far-reaching effects upon her professional and personal life. Between the ages of twenty and thirty-five, professional women make the largest strides up the professional ladder, decide whether to marry and whom, and decide whether to have children.

Professional women need to know

- how to deal with the pitfalls that can damage their careers,
- how to handle office politics,
- what the female-friendly positions are, and what positions have a past history of being unfriendly to women, and
- what issues professional women face that professional men don't face.

Today's women have an endless array of options. They can decide to have children or not to have children. They can decide to be working mothers or become homemakers. Women today can be anything. The problem is, they cannot be everything. Along the road, women have to make choices. Each woman must analyze her own circumstances and make these decisions for herself.

There is only a short period of time between graduating from college and having children. If goals are not reached before having children, it is unlikely that they will be met later on. Keeping the goals you have set for yourself in mind, you will need to carefully plan in order to fit everything in prior to having children (if having children is one of your goals). You may want to

- achieve a specific position (career),
- obtain a license or certification,
- complete a graduate degree,
- reach a specific salary or commission level, or
- be in a family-friendly position (working part

time, flextime, or in a home office) or be so well situated with your employer that you are on solid ground asking to work from a family-friendly position.

All colleges and universities should offer classes to women that teach them how to meet their goals and prepare them for the challenges specifically faced by professional women.

*Planning Your Future: A Guide for Professional Women* explains why women need to consciously recognize what their highest expectations from life are, and how they can set goals that will enable them to achieve those expectations. During this critical decision-making period, women must understand many vital issues that are relevant to their future success and must prepare to meet the challenges therein.

This book also contains the results from a recent study of one hundred women between the ages of twenty-eight and thirty-five who graduated from Villanova University. The study participants were given self-esteem tests and assertiveness tests, and they were questioned about home, work, discrimination, and what they would change if they had it to do all over again. Many interesting findings came out of the study. The study provides a good picture of today's young professional women.

## *Background Information on the Study*

A random sampling program was used to identify study participants. Every woman in the population had an equal chance of being picked for the sample. Appendix 1 contains the demographics of the study participants. It illustrates that the study participants represent today's well-educated women:

- They are single or married,
- have children, want children, or do not want children,
- are homemakers, part-time workers, and full-time workers,
- may or may not have graduate degrees, and
- represent the full range of professions.

However, this study is not representative of minorities. The number of minority women who participated in the study was too small to reach any conclusions about minorities. There is no question that women from minorities face greater obstacles due to their race. In the future, I expect that there will be a number of similar studies specifically for well-educated minority women. In the meantime, women from all minorities can benefit from the information learned from this study.

# PART I

# Achieving Your
# Highest Expectations

# CHAPTER 1

# Today's Climate Is Right

Today, women enjoy working in all types of professions, with varying schedules, and in many different locations. It's simply a matter of finding a match between a career that you will be happy with, a schedule that meets your needs and responsibilities, and a place where you want to work (whether it is in the city, the suburbs, out of your car, or in a home office). There are many options available. It's just a matter of determining which one is right for you and setting out to achieve it.

The current job market is exploding. Unemployment is at an all-time low. Opportunities never seen before exist for individuals seeking positions. Many companies are going the extra mile to attract and retain good professionals.

Some companies offer part-time, flextime, and home office positions as part of a new corporate policy. Other companies that only have full-time in-office employees are willing to make exceptions for good employees who would otherwise leave for positions with more flexible companies.

The technology breakthroughs that have occurred over the past decade have made various scheduling and location options feasible. In many companies, computers, E-mail, and voice mail enable employees to communicate without requiring them to work the same hours at the same time (flextime). In other companies, the information superhighway, cheap fax machines, and improved home phone service (call waiting and conferencing capabilities) have made telecommuting (home office) a viable alternative.

Many women want their future to include a career and motherhood; however, very few women plan and work towards obtaining the best family-friendly position prior to conception. Obtaining a family-friendly position requires planning, time, hard work, compromises, and sacrifices. If you make the investment, you can create a future that lives up to your highest expectations, whatever it may be.

# CHAPTER 2

# Determining What Your Highest Expectations Are

The first step on the road to realizing your dreams is to create a list of your highest expectations from life. Where do you want your future to take you? There are an endless number of questions that you can ask yourself when creating your list of expectations. As a professional woman, you should consider the following questions:

- Do you see yourself having children, and if so, when?
- How many children would you like to have?
- Is it important that you continue working when your children are young?
- What do you want to get out of your career? What needs do you want met?

- How many hours do you envision yourself working every week?
- What type of schedule will suit you?
- Would you be willing to travel for your job?
- What about traveling overnight?
- Does your personality mesh with having a home office? Would there be too many distractions pulling you away? Would you have the discipline to ignore them? Do you need the daily interaction that goes on in an office full of people? Will you miss the camaraderie and closeness that one can experience in an office setting? Do you need the early career mentoring that can only be achieved through one-on-one interaction? Will you be disappointed if your office is given away to someone else who is not working out of a home office?
- How much money do you need to make to be happy?
- Assuming you had more time to spend at home with your children, how much money would satisfy your needs?
- Do you foresee moving or buying a home in the future? How much do you expect to spend?
- Do you need or want to live close to family?
- Are you limited to living in a specific state or city?

Your list of expectations could include:

- providing the best family life for your future children,
- achieving a specific position in your career (such as becoming a partner in your firm),
- achieving a position that provides a sense of accomplishment or meets some other need,
- happiness,
- love,

- good deeds towards others (such as charity work),
- bettering yourself morally (such as becoming less materialistic, less judgmental, or less jealous),
- taking care of a sick relative or friend,
- having time everyday to enjoy your hobby of painting,
- and so on...

Your list of expectations should cover everything you want or need to achieve in your life. Looking back on your life, what do you want to see? Where do you see yourself five, ten, fifteen, fifty years from now? For those of you who know where you want to go in life, this should not be a difficult task. For those of you who aren't so sure, this is going to take some serious soul-searching. Keep in mind that as you travel through life, your expectations will change.

Sort your list of highest expectations in order of importance from most to least important. If you have an expectation that you believe you need to accomplish or your life will be wasted, place it highest on your list. It's perfectly normal if you do not have any expectations that are this important.

# CHAPTER 3

# Setting Goals

Now that you have a prioritized list of what your highest expectations from life are, you will need to determine which goals will enable you to accomplish these expectations. For each expectation, ask yourself, "What goals do I need to accomplish to meet this expectation."

You do not need to be married or dating someone special to start thinking about your future and setting down your goals. It may take a decade to achieve the position that you want, whereas, it may take a total of two years to meet the right person, get married, and have a child. If one of your goals is to be able to work from a home office in a career that you find very fulfilling once you have children, there may not be enough time to achieve all of this after you meet the right person.

As you think about each expectation and the goals necessary to achieve it, fine-tuning of the expectation will occur. For example, assume your expectation is to provide the best family life for your future children. One thousand people with this same expectation could set out to achieve completely different goals, because their definitions of what constitutes "the best family life" would all be different.

If you have an expectation that can be further broken down into meaningful parts — break it down. You will have an easier time finding goals to meet well-defined expectations. For example, I would break down the expectation of "providing the best family life for my children" into the following pieces (your breakdown does not need to agree with mine):

1. My husband and I raising our children together
2. No day care or caregiver outside the family (if possible)
3. Raising the children to
   a. Be happy individuals not relying on others for support
   b. Embrace the morals and values that we hold
   c. Be socially adept at interacting with others
   d. Know and appreciate the fact that they can rely on the family unit and extended family (grandparents, aunts, uncles, etc.)
   e. Be willing and happy to help out family members in times of need
   f. Appreciate and enjoy reading and learning
4. Enjoy daily fun times together
5. Provide a home and material things (food, clothing, money for the movies and college, etc.)

The goals that I would set to attain these expectations would include the following:

1. Working to maintain a strong family relationship
2. Either my husband or me achieving a career that would enable one of us to stay at home with the children, or a combination of both careers and some flexibility (part time, flextime, home office) that would enable us to raise our children
3. Spending quality time with the children
   a. Instilling within the children the importance of becoming productive individuals, then creating the drive for them to achieve it
   b. Teaching our morals and values to our children and setting a good example in practice
   c. Introducing the children to social settings where they can learn to interact with others and providing an ear when tough lessons are learned
   d. Involving the children in family discussions where we rely on each other and our extended family (e.g. grandma picking a child up from school when the child is sick)
   e. Setting a good example of being there for the family and extended family when needed
   f. Taking time out of every day to teach the children and make it an enjoyable experience
4. Taking time to enjoy life with the children on a daily basis
5. Earning more than enough to provide a nice home, necessities, college tuition, some extravagances, and have a nice nest egg left over to do what we want when we retire

Your list of goals will probably be much longer. The above list is based on only one expectation. You will need to prepare a list of goals for each of your highest expectations.

For expectations that are more general and cover more daily activities (such as happiness), evaluate those expectations in relation to achieving your other expectations. For example, assume two of your highest expectations are being happy and becoming a partner in your current law firm. You will need to evaluate whether becoming a partner in your current firm would provide you with happiness. Do you dislike your current position with the firm because of the long hours or because the working atmosphere makes you unhappy (for instance, are there pretentious colleagues you can't stand to be around)? If the answer is yes, realize that it's unlikely that these things will change when you make partner. You should reevaluate your expectation of becoming a partner with this firm. Most likely, there is a firm out there that will have an atmosphere that will meet your needs for a pleasant work environment.

## Working Atmosphere

Many companies have a bad working atmosphere. A bad working atmosphere can be attributed to many sources, including

- disagreements with corporate philosophies,
- personality conflicts with a manager,
- employers who put too much emphasis on the bottom line and burn out their employees, or
- a strong presence of petty individuals and gossips in the workplace.

What you consider a bad atmosphere and what a colleague considers a bad atmosphere may be two separate things. Always do what's best for you.

Do not give up hope, good environments do exist. I have had four employers since graduating from college. I suffered through difficult working atmospheres in my first three positions to obtain the experience and education necessary to obtain a better position with a company that has a very good atmosphere. The company that now employs me is very large (Fortune 500), but remains family oriented. They are truly interested in their employees. They expect hard work and overtime when necessary, but they are careful not to burn employees out. The pace and the stress level is less intense than I had at prior positions, but just as much is accomplished, and the issues I am dealing with are just as important. An atmosphere like this starts at the top of a company and filters down. If a corporate philosophy is not created to make the best working atmosphere for employees, more things will go wrong.

Even companies with corporate policies conducive to providing a pleasant working environment can have offices with bad environments. One bad manager can make any situation difficult, or in extreme cases, intolerable. If you work for this kind of manager, and it looks like you will be under her for years to come, it's time to evaluate the options of transferring to another department or leaving the company. There are a few reasons to stay for a short period of time with a company that makes you unhappy. In some instances, the education and experience may be worth the short-term sacrifice.

Managers who are easily aggravated and who do not handle stress well pass this on to their employees. When I worked for a public accounting firm, there was one partner no one ever wanted to work for because he couldn't keep his stress in check and was always on full boil. It was easy to tell which staff accountants were currently working for this partner, because they were always frazzled.

If you are in a career that attracts individuals with bad attitudes (this is unusual), and the profession requires extensive interaction with this type of individual, a career review may be in order. Bad attitudes are contagious. It's neither something you want to suffer, nor is it something you want to bring home.

# Children?

The most important decision that will affect your goals is whether or not you will have children. Those of you who do not plan to have children will not have the same concerns as the women who plan to have children. Your time frame for achieving your goals need not be as compact. Five percent of the study participants do not expect children to be part of their future. Fifty-nine percent of the study participants already have children.

Most women will bear children at some time in their lives. On the average, eighty percent of women nationally will bear children. As the educational level of women increases,

- the number of children born to these women decreases,
- women wait longer to have their first child, and

| Percentage of Childless Women 35 to 44 Years Old[1] | |
| --- | --- |
| Not a high school graduate | 10.3% |
| High school | 14.4% |
| Some college, no degree | 17.3% |
| Associate's degree | 18.5% |
| Bachelor's degree | 28.1% |
| Graduate or professional degree | 32% |

1. Census Bureau, "Fertility of American Women: June 1995 (Update)." *Current Population Reports* P20-499 (October 1997): Table 2, Part A, 3.

- the number of women who do not have children increases.

No matter what you decide about having children, you can always change your mind (as long as Mother Nature agrees). If you are positive that you will not have children, you can skip the rest of this section and go to the section titled "What makes women happy," beginning on page 33. If you want children to be part of your future, and you do not have any yet, it's time to make plans, so you can begin to follow through on them.

## STAY-AT-HOME MOM OR WORKING MOM

The decision between being a homemaker and a working mom is neither easy nor clear-cut for most women. It's a decision that most women wrestle with.

When the study participants who didn't have any children, but planned to have children in the future were asked "What do you plan on doing when you have children?" their answers were as follows:

- 27% planned to cut back their hours to part time.
- 12% planned to continue working the same as now (after maternity leave).
- 9% would stop working.
- 9% would do other.
- 43% were unsure what they would do.

The fact that 43% of these women were not sure what they would do when they had children should be a wake-up call to most employers. The common conception that women know whether they will continue to work once they have children is incorrect. This study shows that a large group of women do not have their minds made up about whether they will work. The combination of good employees being in high demand, the majority of women having children, and the high cost of employee turnover should entice many companies to be more proactive and flexible in creating family-friendly positions and incentives for employees with children (day care in the building, nursing and pumping rooms, etc.).

Of the mothers in the study,

- 29% were homemakers,
- 36% worked part time (less than forty hours a week),
- 30% worked between forty and fifty hours a week, and
- 5% worked more than fifty hours a week.

Therefore, 65% of these highly educated mothers chose to work part time or were homemakers.

81% of the homemakers worked through their first pregnancy, and 40% of homemakers worked after their first child was born.

Here are the reasons the mothers who work gave for working:

- 44% worked for the money.
- 31% worked because they like what they do for a living.
- 10% worked because their career provides something that they need (power, self-fulfillment, and so on).
- 15% worked for various other reasons, including maintaining skills, the benefits, because they like to work, or because they like their job and it wasn't guaranteed to be there for them if they took time off from work.

If companies want to retain employees who have children, they need to analyze the reasons why mothers work.

The study shows that money is only one reason why women work. More than 50% of the time, highly educated mothers work for reasons other than money. Companies would retain more female employees if they focused on improving the positive factors that influence mothers to work.

Of the mothers who work, 29% of them plan to stop working in the future to become homemakers. Of these mothers,

- 55% plan on doing it after the next child,
- 27% sometime in the near future,
- 9% when they can afford it on their husband's income, and
- 9% are unsure when.

Every woman has different needs, desires, resources, and support. After evaluating the alternatives, many women will determine that their best course of action is to withdraw from the workforce for a period of time to raise their children. Other women will reevaluate their goals and restructure their career path to obtain positions that are more family-friendly (such as working from a home office, or working part time or flextime). If obtaining a family-friendly position is your intention, you will need to invest time in planning and following through (prior to conception). Balancing family and career takes many compromises and sacrifices. Every woman who wants to can find the mix of work and home life that meets her needs, desires, and resources — if she plans and follows through.

### Studies That Have Analyzed the Children of Mothers Who Work and the Children of Mothers Who Stay at Home

For the last forty years, people have been debating whether a child is put at a disadvantage when his or her mother works. I am sad to tell you that the debate still continues.

There have been very few studies covering this issue. The studies conducted so far don't come close to answering the questions most mothers are asking.

The most recent study was conducted by Elizabeth Harvey, a psychologist at the University of Massachusetts at Amherst. It appeared in the March 1999 issue of *Developmental Psychology.* Her study was given a significant amount of media attention. Most major newspapers carried stories interpreting her results.

The writers' preconceived opinions about working mothers significantly impacted the spin placed on this study. Writers who wholeheartedly believed in working mothers wrote articles titled

- "Study Gives Comfort to Working Parents,"
- "Research Shows Child's Development Not Affected by Working Mother,"
- "Good News for Working Mothers,"
- "Working Moms; Surprise! Kids Are Doing Just as Well,"
- "Good News for Working Women Raising Kids,"
- "Kids O.K. If Mom Works," and
- "New Study Finds Children of Working Mothers Are Not Suffering Developmentally Compared to Children Whose Mothers Stay at Home."

Writers who wholeheartedly were against mothers working wrote articles titled

- "Study on Children in Day Care Only a Feel Good Measure,"
- "Family Values on the Roof,"
- "Child Rearing Can't Be Left to Science,"
- "Every Child Knows Moms Are Better Than Day Care,"

- "Parenting Study Defies Common Sense,"
- "Belittling All in the Family," and
- "Working Parents Neglect Most Important Job."

It's hard to believe that all of these articles were written about the same study. The writers who did not look at the study with an open mind (and there were many of these on both sides of the issue) often belittled people holding opposing views. Additionally, they often had the facts wrong. I doubt that many of them actually read the full study prior to writing their articles.

A few of the articles I read suggested that this study was dreamt up by some group with a hidden agenda. I am afraid those writers have been reading too many Tom Clancey novels. Other writers slammed Dr. Harvey because she is a working woman who in their minds would automatically be biased for working mothers. As a working mother, I find that conclusion very offensive. If I was conducting a study to determine whether working while being a mother was detrimental to my children, I would want to find the correct answer, not an answer that made me feel good.

After reading all of these articles with opposing views, I was still left with the question: "If I work, will it have a detrimental effect on my children?" I decided to read Dr. Harvey's study for myself. After reading the study, the point that I was left with was that this study was not attempting to draw any definite conclusions.

The study looked at many variables, but did not look into all the variables and did not look into the various possible outcomes from different combinations of these variables. A few of the variables that would need to be looked at in combination would include income level, marital status, the number of hours the mother worked, the number of hours the father worked, what kind of child care was used, who the child care provider was, the quality of the child care, where the mother worked (home office or outside the house), whether the mother traveled overnight for business, the mother's IQ and educational level, along with many other variables. All of these factors will affect a child and therefore should be considered in any study trying to determine whether a working mother's child is harmed or at a disadvantage.

Dr. Harvey's study relied on a sample that was selected from the same data compilation that was used to pick samples for six other studies on this subject. Even though the same initial data were used to select samples in all of these studies, this study had trouble replicating many of the results from the other studies. In addition, the six other studies had trouble replicating each other's results. Dr. Harvey summed it up best when she stated: "This study had identified one potential positive effect. Future studies are needed..."

Of course, most newspaper articles and news reports did not focus on this point. How many readers can you attract with the headline: "Study Suggests We Need Another Study"? Most of the media coverage focused on the study's figures that indicated that problems initially detected in three- and four-year-old children of working mothers may go away by the time the children reach age twelve. However, after reading the study for myself, I believe that too many variables have not been considered. Moreover, the fact that the results did not replicate those from previous studies suggests that more studies need to be done.

In addition, the study included many mothers whose children were in fact exclusively cared for by their own parents (12% for full-time working mothers and 25% for part-time working mothers). For example, a mother and father can work opposite hours and therefore do not employ an outside caregiver. Also, a significant percentage of the children were watched by other family members or nannies, not day care. Since this study was not based solely on children in day care, I do not believe that the conclusion reached in some articles — "this study concluded there was no harm to children placed in day care" — is supported by the facts at this time. Hopefully, someday there will be studies that will clearly indicate the impact of day care on children one way or another, so parents can have real information to rely on when making parenting decisions.

Doctor Harvey did find that income level and marital status (married versus unmarried mothers) significantly impacted the effects of work on children. Children of poor single mothers appeared to do better when their mothers worked. The study stated that this outcome may be due to less time with mom being balanced by the upside of having enough money to live on. However, that was only an assumption. There could be other reasons; for instance, perhaps the caregivers of the children of low-income single moms had a higher education level than the children's mothers and this tended to rub off. It could also be a combination of several factors.

The study also found that "for married mothers, employment during the first three years was associated with somewhat more behavior problems at ages five to six at a probability level that approached significant."

No matter which side of the issue you are on, it's a hot issue, and I am sure you will be hearing more about it in the future. People tend to feel strongly one way or another. For me, the question still remains: Are children placed at a disadvantage or harmed when their mother works under circumstances similar to mine? For purposes of analysis, knowing the impact of the following factors would be important:

- the mother's background (education and socioeconomic),

- the mother's income level,
- the mother's work situation (full time, part time, home office),
- who the caregiver is (family member, nanny, day care), and
- the amount and quality of time spent with the child.

Only when there is a study that addresses these factors should it be given significant weight by women making the choice to work after having children.

Another question that has not been answered by the studies is, "How will a mother's absence and an alternative caregiver affect the future family unit?" Will it deteriorate or go unchanged? And if the family unit begins to fall apart, will it only fall apart for those who haven't invested their free time in the family?

At this point in time, I have no idea how future studies will turn out; however, I feel secure that even if the average working woman's child is found to be at a disadvantage, mine won't be. I am going to make sure of it. It's my highest priority. I am going to do my best to attend every recital and soccer game. I am going to listen to what my children are saying through actions and speech. If there is the slightest signal that there is a problem developing, it will not go ignored. I am going to do whatever is necessary for my children.

### Homemakers

Homemakers have been given a bad rap and bad press over the last thirty years by the extremists who believe homemakers are subservient oppressed individuals. The homemakers in the Villanova study are neither subservient nor oppressed. They are strong well-educated women who deeply believe that they have made the best decision for their children by taking time off from work to raise them. In fact, 93% of the homemakers from the study believe that women with children who work are jeopardizing their children. The other 7% of the homemakers, who did not say that working mothers are jeopardizing their children, did say that they believe staying at home with their children is the best thing for their children.

The homemakers from the study represent a wide variety of professionals, including those with careers in foreign language, education, business administration, psychology, communications, marketing, nursing, accounting, and engineering. Thirty-eight percent of them have master's degrees. It's wonderful to see such highly educated women taking a hands-on interest in their children. Some short-sighted individuals will view the post-secondary education of homemakers as a waste of time and money. But it's not. The more knowledge a mother has and the stronger her passion for learning, the better chance these values will be instilled in her children.

Recent articles by organizations with agendas that include promoting working mothers at the expense of homemakers have included statements that homemakers are less happy, have lower self-esteem, and have lower assertive skills than the average woman. Later in this book, women's happiness, self-esteem, and assertiveness are discussed in detail. However, I want to shed some light on these specific issues and debunk the myth of the unhappy and weak homemaker right now. Of all the study participants, homemakers were the happiest group on a happiness scale of 1 to 10. They were happier than part-time working mothers, full-time working mothers, women without children, single women, and divorcees. In addition, homemakers had the same average self-esteem scores and assertiveness scores as the average study participants.

Therefore, being a homemaker should not have any stigma associated with it. Well-educated women who leave good careers in order to become homemakers deserve no less respect than career mothers. Some would even argue that they deserve more respect. I'll leave that one up to you.

I have a friend who works part time as a school teacher. She has a three-year-old son and another child due in two months. Last week, she sheepishly told me that she plans to take off a few years from work after this second child is born. I think that's fantastic. The fact that she can do this for her children is wonderful. Her only fear at this point is missing the interaction with other adults. She'll be just fine. She is very outgoing and already heavily involved in a mom's club.

Of all the homemakers from the study, only 20% were at times jealous of mothers who work. Three reasons were listed for the slight envy:

1. I sometimes miss the variety of work.
2. I sometimes miss the interaction with coworkers.
3. I sometimes am envious because working mothers get to go out and have some meaning to their day other than "baby talk."

However, all of the homemakers believe that they have made the right decision by staying at home with their children.

### Working Mothers

Seventy-one percent of working mothers are at times jealous of homemakers. In addition, the more hours a mother works, the higher the rate of jealousy. It breaks down as follows:

- 58% of part-time working mothers are jealous of homemakers,
- 79% of mothers who work forty to fifty hours a week are jealous of homemakers, and
- 100% of mothers who work fifty or more hours a week are jealous of homemakers.

Unlike the homemakers who believe they have made the right decision, the majority of working mothers who said they were jealous of homemakers (especially those who work full time) are not completely sure that they have made the right decision. These women were often in pain over their decisions and were looking for me to either

1. provide a clear-cut solution by telling them to stay at home or work, or
2. make them feel good about their decision to work.

I am afraid that I cannot do either. Every woman's situation is different, and every woman must make the decision for herself. As stated earlier, even the studies flip-flop on what is best for children. In addition, not one of the studies considers what is best for children of well-educated women (homemaker, nanny, day care, etc.).

For those working mothers who want someone to pat them on the back and make them feel better about working, I am not going to do that either. If you have made the right decision, you will know it. There are many articles that tell working mothers not to feel guilty. The main message of the book *She Works/He Works: How Two-Income Families Are Happier, Healthier, and Better-Off* [2] is that working couples should get rid of the guilt. It concluded that two-income families are generally happier and healthier than families in

2. Rosalind Barnett and Caryl Rivers, *She Works/He Works: How Two-Income Families Are Happier, Healthier, and Better-Off* (New York: Harper Collins, 1996). This was a study and a book. Rosalind Barnett is with Radcliffe College and Caryl Rivers is with Boston University.

which only the dad works. It further concludes that working is better for mothers and that working women have higher self-esteem and are less prone to suffer depression than full-time homemakers. They also offer that staying at home has no paycheck as a reward.

I have several problems with this book. First, they make many generalizations about homemakers that are clearly false. The homemakers from the study of Villanova alumni were actually happier than working mothers and had the same average self-esteem as other women. The difference in our results could be that well-educated women who are homemakers do not have the same problems as homemakers who do not have college degrees. Again, I'll leave that up to someone else. The idea that women need a paycheck as a reward is an outrage to the stay-at-home mothers. The homemakers loudly and consistently told me that their reward was their children, and that it was a better reward than any paycheck they could receive.

I also disagree with the theory that working mothers should just give up the guilt. Guilt is defined in *Webster's Dictionary* as "a feeling of responsibility or remorse for some offense, crime, wrong, etc., whether real or imagined." Guilt is a natural human emotion that is there to direct us to do the right thing. When a working mother feels extremely guilty about leaving her child in someone else's care while she works, she needs to analyze the reasons behind the guilt and determine whether it is a real wrong or an imagined one. Again, this is not something that anyone else can decide for these women. It's internally based upon a mother's own beliefs and personal situation.

Personally, I hold no guilt about working under my circumstances. I work out of a home office. My mother watches my daughter downstairs in my house during the day. I can take a break and play with my daughter any time I want. My mother is wonderful with her. My daughter will be a better person for having spent time with her. My husband, my daughter, and I spend endless hours together when we are not working. My working situation is not at odds with my values.

However, if I had to work outside the home or if someone other than my mother was my daughter's caregiver, based upon my own values, I would have a natural guilt that I was not doing right by my daughter. If either of those two situations occurred, I would stop working to be at home. However, I do not expect other women who work outside the home or have non-family members watching their children to stop working based upon my beliefs. Women must determine their own boundaries.

Guilt is our internal mechanism for telling us that we may be doing something that goes against our values. Guilt is not something that should be ignored. If you find that you are feeling guilty on a regular basis, analyze it and find out the true reason for it. If you truly believe you are doing the right thing, the guilt should disappear. If the guilt persists, your internal conscience is telling you that there is a piece of you that believes you are not doing the right thing.

If you are considering becoming a homemaker, there are many good books and organizations that can help. The not-for-profit organization Mothers & More (previously called FEMALE: Formerly Employed Mothers at the Leading Edge) is dedicated to helping women make the transitions from work to stay-at-home mom and from stay-at-home mom back to work. You can find them at www.femalehome.org.

### The Best-Laid Plans Can Change

Once you have made your decision to work or not work, remember that circumstances change and the best-laid plans should bend to accommodate those changes:

- A mother who has to work full time for monetary reasons may all of a sudden be able to stay at home because her husband was given a big promotion.
- A mother who was at home with her children sees her last child off to first grade and finds herself wanting to reenter the workforce earlier than planned.
- A mother who decided to stay at home with her children until they reached school age may find that when her children are all attending school, there are still too many high-priority demands on her time for her to reenter the workforce.
- A mother who decided to go back to work after her first child was born couldn't stand the time away from her child and gives up her job to be a stay-at-home mom.

### Stick with a Decision That Is Right for You

Once you have searched your soul, and you have made the decision to either be a stay-at-home mom or a working mom (full time, part time, flextime, or from a home office), don't second-guess your decision based upon what others will think. You've put a lot of thought into the decision, and you've made the best decision for you and your family. There are well-meaning family members, friends, and colleagues who will disagree with your decision. You cannot make everyone happy.

If you decide to stay at home, you may hear opinions from

- family members who have made sacrifices for your education,
- friends who are shocked and surprised because they thought of you as such a "career woman,"

- individuals who have aspirations about where your career might lead to in the future, or
- colleagues who have a financial interest or work-related interest in your staying on as an employee.

If you decide to continue working (whether it is full time, part time, flextime, or from a home office), you will hear opinions from family members, friends, and colleagues who believe that the only way to raise your children is for you to be at home full time with them. The American public, which touts a woman's right to have a career, generally holds the belief that you cannot be a good mother and hold down a professional career at the same time. However, if you become a working mother, you are not alone: 68% of U.S. mothers with school-age children work and 58% of mothers with children under the age of three work.

## CHILD CARE

If you made the decision to continue working, the next important decision you will need to make is what kind of child care will be acceptable to you.

Questions you need to ask yourself:

- Who would you allow to care for your children while you are working?
- What are your feelings and thoughts about day care and nannies?

If you are interested in the one-on-one care from a nanny, speak with your friends who have had nannies about their experiences and what they would change. Questions to ask yourself regarding a nanny include:

- Would you be willing to have this caregiver watch your children in your house?

**OUACHITA TECHNICAL COLLEGE**

- Would you mind your child going to the nanny's house?

If day care may be an option, speak with your friends who have used day care about their experiences. There are many good day care facilities. It's your responsibility to research local day cares and find your child a good one.

Many books and articles are dedicated to telling you how to find the best day care or nanny. You should learn how to perform a background check and verify references. Stop in at unexpected times and evaluate the facility's cleanliness, safety features (or lack of them), how the children currently attending are acting (crying, being ignored by caregivers, being talked to too harshly), and staffing ratio. Could someone walk off with a child who was not their own? Do the research and make sure your child is with a good caregiver.

Another variation in child care is for the husband and wife to work alternating hours, so that no caregiver is needed. We have friends that do this. The husband works forty hours Monday through Friday and the wife works two ten hour shifts every Saturday and Sunday. This alternative has the benefit that the parents watch and raise their own children. However, the compromises and sacrifices involved in such a scenario are great.

Hiring an au pair is another option. I am sure that you are all aware of the incident involving British au pair Louise Woodward. Despite that incident, I know people who have been very happy with their au pairs. Hiring an au pair may be a good option for you. Just do your research. Personally, I could never have someone else live in my house. I hold my privacy and quiet time with my family very dear and wouldn't want to lose that.

*The Unofficial Guide to Childcare* by Ann Douglas is a wonderful reference for navigating the world of nannies, au pairs, and day care centers.

## BUYING A HOME CLOSE TO FAMILY

When you are looking for a house to buy, do not rule out moving close to family. Being close to family when you have children is a luxury. Do not underestimate its importance. I have several friends who wish they had bought houses closer to their families now that they have children. Close does not necessarily mean moving next door. If your employment is in the area and you plan to have children, there are very few reasons not to move close to family. A few of the reasons are that

- your family is a nightmare, and you need to stay as far away as possible,
- your family lives in a neighborhood that you cannot afford, and
- your family lives in an area that would not meet your goals (they live in a suburb, and you want to live in the city; they live in a row home, and you want to live in a single family home, etc.).

There is less motivation to move close to family if your parents will not or cannot fully participate in your children's lives. Such reasons include:

- your parents may already have fifteen grandchildren and do not participate very enthusiastically with the ones they already have, or
- your parents are not physically able to participate with your children.

If the main reason holding you back from buying a house close to family is fear, rethink the situation. Many women worry about moving too close to their parents or their in-laws for fear that

1. they will not get any privacy because the family will be over all the time;

2. the family will be too critical of how they are raising the children or their lives in general;
3. they'll go crazy because they can only handle their parents or in-laws in small doses; or
4. their own opinions and thoughts will hold less weight than their in-laws' opinions in their husbands' minds because the husbands are predisposed to making their parents happy.

If one (or all) of the above four fears is holding you back from moving close to family, ask yourself whether you believe they will be good grandparents. If the answer is yes, think hard and long before allowing these fears to influence your decision about where to move. It's in the best interest for your children to live close to their grandparents. It's in your best interest to have family you can rely on nearby. If you don't move close, you will be taking a very special opportunity away from your children.

Has there been a pattern of previous behaviors that would lead a reasonable person to steer away from moving close to your children's grandparents? In most instances, you will find your fear is unfounded. But even if there is a realistic concern that one of the four above will take place, if you are strong and your relationship with your husband is strong, you can handle it.

Most grandparents never want you to think that they are too involved or too overbearing. If an incident takes place that concerns you, bring the issue and your concerns up to the grandparent right away. Do not let it fester. When you do approach the subject, do not do it in an adversarial way. You are your children's parent. Generally, if you tell your mother-in-law how important she is to the family and how you appreciate everything she does for you, but at the present time you are feeling a little smothered (or whatever your concern is), she'll probably be surprised, and the two of you can work it out from there.

If the problem that arises is that your husband places more value on his family's opinions than yours, it's time for a discussion with your husband. The problem doesn't lie with his parents, it lies between the two of you. Talk with your husband about your concerns and how to make things better going forward.

If your family is willing to move close to you wherever you locate, or if your family expects to move in the near future, buying a home close to them is moot.

# What Makes Women Happy?

When the study participants were originally asked to rate how happy they were, I didn't think there would be a pattern. Boy, was I surprised when a pattern began to emerge.

The participants were asked, "On a scale of 1 to 10, how happy are you with the way things are going in your life" (10 being extremely happy and 1 being totally disappointed). The average score among the participants was an 8.2.

## MARRIAGE, CHILDREN & STAYING AT HOME

Here is a breakdown of scores between the various groups:

- homemakers averaged 8.9
- married with children, working part time (less than forty hours a week), averaged 8.6
- married with children, working full time (more than thirty-nine hours a week), averaged 8.3
- married and no kids averaged 7.9
- singles averaged 7.7
- divorced with kids averaged 6.5

There is a clear pattern that women who are married, have children, and work the fewest hours are the happiest. As the number of hours of work increases, or if a married woman has no children, or if a woman is not married, her happiness score generally goes down. Keep in mind that this is just an average. Some homemakers rated their happiness as a 7 and some married with kids working full time rated it as a 10. In addition, anyone who rates their life as an 8 or higher is doing pretty well.

There have been other happiness studies conducted in the past that agree with these findings. A 1998 study found that men and women who remained married reported a significantly higher level of happiness than those who remained single. It also showed that those who separated or divorced became miserable.[3] A 1992 Canadian study found that professional women who put career above all else were less content than professional women who took time out to marry and have children. This study specifically focused on professional women in medicine, law, engineering, and accounting. The study found that married professional women with children were the happiest, followed by married professional women without children, and then least happy were the single professional women without children.[4]

Back in 1972 a study incorrectly found that marriage was bad for women. Sociologist Jessie Bernard published a study stating that married men were better off than single men on four measures of psychological distress (depression, neurotic symptoms, phobic tendency, and passivity), and that married women scored worse on these traits than single women.[5] Her study became part of the 1970s conventional wisdom, even though no other researcher was able to replicate the findings, and many

3. This study was published in November 1998 in the *Journal of Family Issues* by two psychologists at the University of Wisconsin, Nadine Marks and James Lambert.

4. Ethel Roskies, presented at the Conference on Workplace Stress, which was sponsored by the National Institute for Occupational Safety and Health and the American Psychological Association, Washington (November, 1992). A study conducted by a University of Montreal psychologist.

5. Jessie Bernard, *The Future of Marriage* (Yale University Press, 1972). Jessie Bernard died in 1996 at the age of 93.

had stated that the evidence was flawed. At the time, the belief was that marriage was an oppressive institution for women. Only extremists hold this opinion today.

A study released by sociologist Catherine Ross in 1993 concluded that, on the average, the least depressed women are those who have a job and no children and among the most depressed are those who stay at home with their children. She said, "Any plea to return to the traditional family of the 1950s is a plea to return wives and mothers to a psychologically disadvantaged position in which husbands have much better mental health than wives."[6] That's ridiculous. Being a homemaker is a great option for those who can afford it. If a homemaker is in a psychologically disadvantaged position to her husband, it is not due to her choice to become a homemaker. Women are only at a disadvantage or subservient to husbands when they allow it to happen. Women choose the husbands they marry, and some women chose to be walked on by their husbands. It's all a matter of choice.

A small facet of marriage is the struggle for power. It's generally an unconscious struggle that takes place during the first few years of marriage. After the first few years, the boundaries are generally established, and hopefully, a balance is achieved. However, if women do not handle the struggle appropriately, they can end up giving their power to their husbands. For example, assume a mother tells her son every time she finds him doing something wrong that she is going to tell his father as soon as he gets home. This mother is freely giving up her power to her husband. She is essentially telling the son that the father's opinion and disciplinary actions are more important than hers, and that she does not have the power to handle the situation herself.

---

6. Catherine Ross, paper presented at the annual meeting of the American Association for the Advancement of Science, Boston (February 1993). Catherine Ross is a sociologist at the University of Illinois.

These power struggles happen every day in marriages. When my husband and I were first married, my husband saw that I made an out-of-character purchase on the credit card. I had purchased a Dana Buchman suit. He questioned the need for the purchase. There were three possible responses I could have given him. First, I could have said, "Sorry, won't happen again." That would have been the really wimpy response. Second, I could have lied and told him how important the suit was and tried to win the sympathy support. Again, this response would have set a pattern of being questioned on future purchases. Third, I could have sat him down and explained that he had no right to question the reasonableness of my purchases because

- I don't splurge often;
- my spending habits were not putting us in debt;
- I am good at saving money;
- I make as much money as he does; and
- I don't question the reasonableness of his golf trips.

I took the third option, and he hasn't questioned my purchases since. Of course, if I had been a homemaker, I would have stuck to the same response but eliminated the fact that I made as much as him. I probably would have added to the argument that we were in a partnership and that my work enabled him to provide the income for the family, and therefore I had the same freedom, as he did, to spend the money.

Not giving up your power is very important. Weak women tend to give up their power in both marriage and business. Being weak is a choice.

## HOURS WORKED

Of the women (with kids and without) who worked more than fifty hours a week, the average happiness score was a

7.8. On average, the more hours a woman worked, the less happy she was.

## INCOME?

The study found no correlation between women's happiness and the amount of income they earned.

## Maslow's Hierarchy of Needs

According to Maslow's Hierarchy of Needs, human needs follow a specific pattern. After one level of needs has been fulfilled and secured, an individual's needs jump up to the next level. The bottom two levels are the basic needs for survival, and the top three levels are growth needs. Income fulfills a survival need. Once an income sufficient to meet basic survival needs is met, it is no longer needed beyond that. This explains why there is a strong correlation between income and happiness in poor countries. But there is little correlation in well-off countries such as the United States.

A study by Ed Diener, a psychologist at the University of Illinois, found that when you are in middle-class America and living in the suburbs, money probably cannot buy you much more happiness. If you are poor and in Calcutta, money can buy you happiness.[7]

## SELF-ESTEEM & ASSERTIVENESS

One factor is more important than marriage, children, and hours worked in affecting a woman's happiness. That factor is self-esteem. Women in the top self-esteem category had an average happiness score of 9.5. Women in the top assertiveness category had an average score of 8.5. Therefore, very good assertive skills increased a woman's chance of being happy, but having good self-esteem almost guaranteed it.

Ed Diener's study also found a significant correlation between self-esteem and happiness in the United States.[8] Self-esteem and assertiveness are discussed further in Chapter 5.

## WOMEN WHO WOULD NOT MAKE CHANGES IN THE CHOICES THEY HAVE MADE

When the women in the study were asked what they would change if they had it all to do over again, 32% responded that they would not change a thing. Of these women, there was an average happiness rating of 8.6. Therefore, the women who believed they had made the correct decisions in their lives also tended to be happier.

## PROFESSIONS

Several professions have a reputation for using up their professionals and then discarding them, while other professions

---

7. Sally Weeks, "A Social Science Puts Emotions on the Map," *World Paper* (February 1998): 11.

8. Ibid.

are viewed as more employee-friendly. In the study, there were very few study participants who worked full time in the same profession. Therefore, the below information is from a very small sample and should only be used to stimulate further studies on the subject.

| Average Happiness Factors for Full-Time Work | |
|---|---|
| Teachers | 9.2 |
| Attorneys | 8.0 |
| Nurses (including nurse practitioners) | 7.0 |

This preliminary review indicates that there may be a correlation between a woman's happiness and the profession she chooses. Further research is needed to verify this hypothesis.

## SUMMARY

Women are almost guaranteed great happiness when they have good self-esteem. Women who are married, have children, and work the fewest hours are also strongly inclined to be happier. Women who are happy with the choices that they made in their lives and women with good assertiveness skills also had higher happiness scores.

Income had no impact on happiness for these women. The study also resulted in a hypothesis that a woman's chosen profession may also significantly impact her happiness. However, this hypothesis will need to be tested with further studies.

Overall, the women had a happiness score of an 8.2. In the realm of things, that's very good. In addition, these results were only averages. There were women who did not possess the factors that would indicate higher happiness, yet they were very happy. Let's face it, happiness is also a little dependent on genetics. Everyone knows at least one person that was born happy and has smiled every day since.

## Evaluate Your Answers

Now that you have a list of your highest expectations from life and a list of your goals, reevaluate both documents. Will you be happy if you meet these goals? Is there anything missing? Are your expectations realistic?

Your list should reflect you as an individual and who you want to be in the future. These are your choices, your goals, your priorities, and your values. If you are married, it's important that you discuss these lists with your spouse. Marriage is a partnership. Remember your husband has goals of his own, and they may not always match yours. Discuss solutions to any goals that are at odds and keep an open mind.

Your next step will be to reevaluate your goals in light of several limiting factors. Chapter 4 is dedicated to the resources that could limit your goals. Chapter 5 is devoted to the other intangible items impacting your goals.

# Resources That Could Limit Your Goals

## Time & Attention

The number one resource that people are lacking today is time. Whenever I am asked what I need, my response is always more time. I'd like additional time to spend with my daughter, additional time to work on projects, and additional time for housework. Actually, I am always behind on housework. My family and my marriage come first, work comes second, and housework always comes in last. We are only given so much time, and that's it. It's a very precious commodity.

Prioritizing your lists will help determine what goals are important enough to take up your valuable time. One woman may have a list that puts her family first and her career second (for monetary purposes). If she has any remaining time, she may decide to spend it on her hobby of painting. Of course, there is never enough time if you work and are raising children. A goal such as painting will be shortchanged while children are young. But as the children grow, she will be able to bring painting more fully back into her life. One option is to make painting something mother and children enjoy doing together.

If you are spending time on a goal, but the goal is not receiving your full attention, the goal may be shortchanged, and it may never be fully accomplished. For example, if your goal is to take time to enjoy life with your children on a daily basis, and you spend that time every day with the children zoning out in front of the TV when you get home from work, are you truly meeting your goal? If you have a goal for your children to become good individuals, you not only need to spend time with your children, you also need to pay attention to being a good role model. If a goal is based on achieving one of your highest expectations, it's worth being done with your full attention.

Your children also have a limited amount of time to accomplish their schoolwork and their other goals. It's your responsibility to make sure they are best using their own time as well. Having time to play is a big part of learning. Not everything has to be a structured activity. Many children are involved in various activities such as sports, the scouts, religious organizations, and playing instruments. Structured activities can be great, but in moderation. Make sure your children have enough unstructured time. Carefully keep track of the time required for structured activities. For example, your daughter may be involved in three activities that require her to sell items for fundraisers (cookies, wrapping paper, and booster stickers). Is your child learning more from selling three times this year versus once? Does she enjoy selling, or would she rather be at the park playing basketball? If you can afford it, instead of letting your child participate in two of the fundraisers, make a donation to the organizations for the amount they reasonably would make as profit off your child. These types of selling activities can also take up a portion of the parent's time — time that could be spent on other activities.

As a family's income increases over the years, the family may be able to free up some time by paying someone else to do chores. When my husband and I first moved into our house, we learned that previous owners had painted over several layers of wallpaper. Our goal has been to renovate one room a year. My husband has always been put in charge of the tedious task of scraping the walls. It usually takes him several weeks. The first few years he did it himself, but this last year we paid someone to come in and scrape the room. The scraping was completed in one day with the proper industrial equipment and a team. As our income increases, there are several other tedious tasks that we are going to be happy to pay others to do. The one hundred hours or more it would have taken my husband to scrape this last room compared with the amount we paid a company to come in and do it for us was well worth it. This was a chore he disliked, and he was happy to give it up.

On the other hand, as you move up the pay scale, there will be household chores that are no longer worth your time, but you may not want to give up control over those chores. This is especially difficult for those of us who come from families that are not used to paying others to do household chores. I don't want someone else cleaning my house, and my husband doesn't want someone else mowing our yard. It will never be done the way we want. However, we do not have the time to do everything, so we've had to compromise. I'd rather compromise and give up vacuuming than give up time with my daughter. Of course, there are many people who dislike household work and would be happy handing this work over to someone else as their family income increases. It's interesting to note that contrary to popular belief, a new study released by Thomas J. Stanley in his best-selling book *The Millionaire Mind* found that millionaires may be frugal, but most do not take on do-it-yourself projects.[9]

Simplify your life back to the basics. Get rid of the unnecessary nuisances. For example, many people receive daily phone calls from companies that want to sell them their products. These calls unnecessarily pull you away from whatever you are doing. There are two things you should do to reduce the number of these calls. First, tell every salesperson that calls that "we don't accept solicitation at this number — please take us off your list." Second, send a note to The Direct Marketing Association telling them to add you to the list of individuals who do not want unsolicited phone calls. The note containing your name, address, and phone number should be sent to The Direct Marketing Association, Telephone Preference Service, P.O. Box 9014, Farmingdale, NY 11735-9014. These two steps will not eliminate all calls, but you will see a significant reduction. If you want to stop junk mail, write to The Direct Marketing Association, Mail Preference Service, Box 9008, Farmingdale, NY 11735-9008.

# Money

Money is the resource that makes achieving your goals that much easier. If you have money, you have more options.

Those of us who weren't born wealthy, didn't marry a millionaire, aren't expecting a large inheritance, and haven't saved a fortune since college graduation need to look at our goals in terms of whether they will require a

---

9. Thomas J. Stanley, *The Millionaire Mind* (Andrews McMeel Publishing, 2000).

monetary expenditure and how that will fit in with our projected income. For example, when a woman compares the options of being an at-home mom with being a working mother, if her income (after taxes, travel expense to work, and other work related expenses) is close to the amount that it would cost her for child care, she may decide to stay at home. Other monetary decisions that may impact your goals include:

- how close you are to vesting in your company's match to your retirement account,
- whether your family's health care is covered by your employer or your husband's,
- whether as a teacher, you are close to receiving tenure, and
- whether part-time work will keep you on track monetarily to meet your other goals.

Money is a factor that affects many goals. Analyze your goals in relation to the cost and monetary benefit of obtaining them. Assume a woman has a goal of attending graduate school, but she cannot afford the tuition if she stops working. A feasible solution may be to attend night school.

## WHAT ARE THE MOST IMPORTANT FACTORS IMPACTING A WOMAN'S COMPENSATION?

For comparison purposes, this section only compares the salaries of study participants who work full time (forty or more hours per week). Homemakers and part-time workers are not included in these calculations.

Study participants' earnings:

- 2% made under $25,000
- 33% made $25,000–$50,000
- 40% made $50,000–$75,000

- 16% made $75,000–$100,000
- 9% made over $100,000

In order to easily compare the factors that impact earnings, $75,000 was chosen as the threshold. All the following factors are analyzed by determining what percentage of the participants with a specific factor earned over $75,000. **In the study, 25% of the full-time professional working women earned more than $75,000 a year.** This was calculated by adding the 16% and 9% from the list above.

How much a woman earns is not reflective of her worth as a human being. Striving for monetary goals is not necessarily a worthwhile goal in itself. That said, women are interested in income, and $75,000 was a good figure to use for comparison purposes. If you make less than $75,000, do not get down. Most Americans do not earn $75,000.

### Happiness?

As stated earlier, there was no correlation between happiness and the amount of income earned by these study participants.

### Age?

**There was no correlation between age and income.** The fact that the youngest study participants were twenty-eight years old and many of them already had seven years of experience in their fields suggests that experience after seven plus years did not significantly increase a woman's chance of moving into a higher earnings category ($25,000 increments).

### Switching Employers To Increase Salary/Compensation

28% of the women who switched employers to increase their salaries/compensation made over $75,000. 20% of the women who did not switch employers to increase their salaries/compensation made over $75,000 a year.

### Male/Female/Coed Professions

32% of the women who worked in co-ed professions made over $75,000 annually. It was 18% of those working in men's professions and 13% of those working in female professions.

### Graduate Degrees

33% of those with graduate degrees made over $75,000 a year. (52% of full-time workers had graduate degrees, compared with 47% of all the study participants.)

### Women Who Didn't Want To Have Children in Their Future

40% of the women who did not want to have children in their future made over $75,000 a year. The reason why women who do not want to have children tend to make more money than women with children is because they can focus more fully on their careers. The U.S. Department of Labor reported in April 1999 that of all female wage and salary workers, 25.8% worked less than thirty-five hours per week compared to 10.7% of all the men.[10] On the average women work fewer hours than men due to the choices women make for their children. In addition, 69% of the Villanova study mothers had their professional goals change once they had children. Women who do not want children do not have their professional goals change due to the introduction of children.

---

10. U.S. Department of Labor, Bureau of Statistics, *Highlights of Women's Earnings in 1998*, Report 928 (April 1999).

### Hours Worked

**47% of those who worked more than fifty hours per week made over $75,000.** However, only 16% of those who worked between forty and fifty hours per week made over $75,000 a year.

### Assertiveness

An assertiveness test was given to each study participant. Assertiveness is discussed in detail later in the book. **50% of the women in the top assertiveness category made over $75,000.** However, only 12% of the women in the lowest assertiveness category made over $75,000 a year.

### Self-Esteem

A self-esteem test was given to each participant. Self-esteem is also discussed in detail later in the book. **60% of the women who had high self-esteem scores made over $75,000 a year.** Since 60% of the women with high self-esteem made over $75,000 a year, but only 25% of the average participants made over $75,000, it shows that self-esteem is a very significant factor impacting women's earnings.

### Combining Self-Esteem & Assertiveness

**75% of the women who scored in both the top 25% of self-esteem and the top 25% of assertive skills among the participants made more than $75,000 a year.** Therefore, a combination of high self-esteem and high assertive skills were the most significant factors impacting women's earnings. However, there was little or no correlation between high assertive scores and high self-esteem scores. Therefore, when a woman scored high in one skill, it did not significantly increase the chance she had scored high in the other skill.

### Professions

The profession that a woman chooses also significantly impacts her potential future earnings. Some professions pay well and others do not.

According to the Web site www.wageweb.com, here are the national averages for a few selected professions:

| Selected National Average Incomes | | |
|---|---|---|
| **Position Title** | **Mean Average Salary as of 1/1/00** | **Mean Average Max. Salary** |
| Social Worker | $33,272 | $38,203 |
| Sup. Social Work | $42,815 | $46,388 |
| RN | $44,523 | $51,244 |
| Nurse Manager | $57,193 | $64,999 |
| Chemical Engineer | $61,211 | $75,861 |
| Chem. Eng. Sup. | $82,218 | $91,080 |
| Information Syst. Mgr. | $98,114 | $123,100 |

As you can see, there is a large difference between the income potential of the various professions.

Women are no longer limited, nor are they discouraged from entering male-dominated fields. In fact, many male-dominated professions will soon become female-dominated professions as today's female college graduates matriculate into the workforce.

In the United States, women earn 56% of the bachelor's degrees and 57% of the master's degrees. They earn the majority of degrees in the previously male-dominated fields of biological sciences, journalism, pharmacy, veterinary medicine, and psychology. They account for 48% of the bachelor's degrees earned in business management.[11] Women account for 46% of all first-year medical students and 45% of the entrants into law school.

---

11. U.S. Department of Education, National Center for Education Statistics, *Integrated Postsecondary Education Data System, Completions Survey.* Table was prepared June 1999 for degrees conferred in 1997.

Women are still the majority in teaching, nursing, and liberal arts studies. Most women are still not interested in entering the fields of architecture and engineering.

Based on the facts that

- more women than men are entering college,
- the professions that women enter are no longer limited, and
- more women than men are still choosing to enter fields that pay less,

it is clear that many women give more weight to their interest in a field than to the potential earnings when choosing a profession. That's great. Life is much easier when you like what you do for a living. However, women should be aware of the earnings outlook for the professions that they choose.

### What Are Others in Your Profession Earning?

You need to keep abreast of what others in your chosen profession are earning. If you are in college, it's important to have information that will help you determine your potential future earnings. If you are already in the workforce, it's important to know how your earnings compare to the earnings of others in your profession.

Several organizations publish salary information. Many of them put it on the Internet. Here are two free Web sites that contain salary information:

- www.jobsmart.org/tools/salary/sal-prof.htm has links to more than 300 salary surveys. For example, if you are researching psychology salaries, you would find links to three salary surveys just for psychology professionals.
- www.wageweb.com lists the average minimum

salary, the mean average salary, and the average maximum salary for more than 160 positions.

It is important to look at as many salary sources as possible. The more narrowly the job categories are defined, the more accurately the salaries will reflect your specific position. For example, the mean salary for an Accountant I as of the first of January, 2000 was $33,907 (www.wageweb.com), but a top partner with a Big 5 accounting firm may earn several hundred thousand a year. Studies that explain the calculations behind their salary summaries will also be more meaningful than those that do not.

There are hundreds of other salary surveys on the Web. Take time to surf the ones that are relevant to you. I am assuming that you are Internet savvy. If you aren't, it is time you took a class or read a book. Not knowing how to use the Internet will put you behind the eight ball in your personal and professional life.

Make sure whatever sources you use to obtain salary comparison data is up to date. A 1995 survey may no longer accurately reflect salary levels.

Several salary surveys discuss the wage gap between men and women. Due to the fact that most of the wage gap is due to choices that women make rather than discrimination, read such surveys with the knowledge you obtain from the section of this book titled "Discrimination."

For those of you in very specialized careers, there may be very little relevant salary information for you on the Internet. A good starting point would be contacting the organization that represents professionals in your specialty. Often, such organizations will conduct salary surveys of their members every few years. Another good place for information is on-line job advertisements. It's always informative to learn what others are willing to pay for similar positions. How to search on-line job databases is discussed later in this book under "Research the Outlook for Your Profession," beginning on page 78.

**Summary of Factors Impacting Income**

25% of the study participants who worked full time earned more than $75,000 a year.

- Switching employers to increase salary/compensation increased that figure to 28%.
- Working in a co-ed profession increased a woman's chance of earning more than $75,000 a year to 32%.
- A graduate degree increased that figure to 33%.
- Women who do not want children increased it to 40%.
- Working more than fifty hours a week increased it to 47%.
- Women in the top assertiveness category increased it to 50%.
- Having high self-esteem increased that figure to 60%.
- Study participants who possessed a combination of good assertive skills and good self-esteem had a 75% chance of earning more than $75,000 a year.

The eight factors that impact a woman's potential earnings, in order of importance:

1. profession chosen
2. self-esteem
3. assertiveness
4. hours worked
5. whether a woman does not want children in her future
6. graduate degrees
7. co-ed profession versus male/female professions
8. switching employers to increase salary/compensation

If a woman is interested in increasing her income potential, she may want to look into improving some of these factors. Later in the book, how to increase one's self-esteem and assertiveness are discussed in greater detail. The number of hours worked is a quality-of-life issue. The decision whether to have children should not be affected by how much money a woman wants to make, unless there is a question whether there will be enough money to support her children. The impact a graduate degree has on earnings depends on the profession. Do your research first.

### The Seven Study Participants
### Who Earned More Than $100,000 Annually

There were seven study participants who earned more than $100,000 annually. I was very surprised to find attorneys and high-end finance positions missing from this list. See the table on the next page.

Of the eight factors mentioned on the previous page that impact a woman's potential earnings, study participants who earned more than $100,000 a year possess more of these factors than the average study participant does. Here are the statistics for the seven women who earned more than $100,000 annually:

- All of these individuals worked in professions that provided the opportunity to be paid well.
- Their average self-esteem score was higher than the average participant's score.
- Their assertiveness score was significantly higher than the average participant's.
- 57% of them worked more than fifty hours a week. This is much higher than the 19% of all participants who worked more than fifty hours a week and were not homemakers.

- 14% never expected to have children. Whereas, 5% of all the participants never expected to have children.
- 43% had graduate degrees. This percentage was a little higher than the average participants'.
- 86% worked in co-ed professions. This was much higher than the 48% working in co-ed professions from all participants. 14% of those earning more than $100,000 worked in predominantly male professions. None worked in female professions.
- 71% had switched employers to increase their salaries, whereas only 42% of the total study population had switched employers to increase their salaries.

## Background Information for Study Participants Earning More Than $100,000 Annually

| Profession | Undergraduate Degree | Graduate Degree | Hours Worked in Week |
|---|---|---|---|
| Market/Advertising Researcher | Marketing | —— | 50+ hours |
| Sales Management | Marketing | —— | 50+ hours |
| Sales | Economics | MBA | 50+ hours |
| IS Manager | Computer Science | MBA | 50+ hours |
| Pharmaceutical Research and Development Mgr. | Chemistry | Organic Chemistry | 40–50 hours |
| Bank Manager | Sociology | —— | Part Time |
| Small Business Owner (Service Industry) | English and Communications | —— | Part Time |

Overall, more of these women displayed the personal attributes and behaviors that tend to increase the chance of a higher income. These included higher self-esteem, higher assertiveness, working more than fifty hours a week, no desire for children, graduate degrees, co-ed professions, and switching employers to increase their salaries. However, not one of them possessed all of these traits.

Here are some relevant statistics on the participants who made over $100,000 annually. This has been provided for those of you who love details.

- They ranged in age from twenty-eight to thirty-five.
- 29% of them were single, and 71% were married.
- 57% of them worked at least occasionally from a home office. This is much higher than the 27% figure found among all working study participants.
- 29% had flexible hours. This figure is very close to the 31% found among all working study participants.
- 57% switched employers to get out of dead-end positions, versus 40% of the total study population.
- 43% of them had children.
- 57% would not change a thing in the past. This was higher than the 32% from all participants.

## *How Much Do Children Cost?*

### Maternity and Delivery Costs

According to the Health Insurance Association of America, hospital and doctor bills associated with an uncomplicated delivery average $6,378. On the average, C-sections cost $10,638.[12] In addition, where you live and which hospital

---

12. Health Insurance Association of America, *Source Book of Health Insurance Data* (Washington, D.C.: 1996).

you deliver in can significantly impact the costs. They can easily double in some areas. However, couples with health insurance may pay less than $1,000.

If you or your spouse is employed, there is no good reason for you not to have health insurance. Assuming you have the money to pay for food, clothing, and shelter, the next highest priority should be health care (followed by education). Health insurance should come before VCR's, cellular phones, beepers, concert tickets, and vacations.

The Census Bureau reported that 16.3% of Americans (44.3 million people) had no health insurance in 1998. Most of those individuals were in low-income families. Of those households with incomes less than $25,000, 25.2% were uninsured. However, 8.3% of households with annual incomes of $75,000 or more were uninsured. There is no excuse for families that earn more than $75,000 a year not to have insurance.

Many employers pay a substantial portion of their employees' health insurance. If the company that you are interviewing with does not provide health insurance supplementation, continue to seek employment with other companies. Today's job market is too good to shortchange yourself on benefits.

Companies range in supplementing these premiums from contributing nothing per employee to paying the entire premium. Most employees do not realize how much companies pay to reduce their portion of the premium. Total premiums per family per month average $459 with HMO's, $514 with preferred provider organizations, and $529 with traditional insurance.[13] When comparing job offers, make sure you take into account the entire package being offered, including health insurance and the employer's matching contribution to the retirement plan.

---

13. A survey conducted by New York–based benefits consultant Towers Perrin in 1999.

The four employers that I have worked for have paid the majority of their employees' health insurance premiums. My portion of my health insurance premium has ranged from a high of $150 a month to a low of $35 a month.

## The Cost of Child Care

The high cost of child care is often a factor that causes parents to decide to stay at home with their children. According to *The Unofficial Guide to Childcare* by Ann Douglas, professionally trained nannies cost $24,000 to $48,000 per year on top of room and board. Untrained nannies (baby-sitters) cost between $5 to $10 an hour ($10,000 to $21,000 annually).[14] If you expect to go this route when you have children, find out the average cost in your area. Ask your friends what they're paying. Your plans may change based upon the cost.

If nannies are too expensive, but you want or need to continue to work, day care may be your answer. The Children's Defense Fund reports that full-time day care costs average between $4,000 and $10,000 a year, with younger children being more expensive. If you are interested in day care, find out the average cost by calling the day cares in your area. Day care can be costly and your plans may change accordingly.

Au pairs receive approximately $120 a week, plus room and board, plus $500 towards education, plus the au pair program may require an additional $4,000 in order for you to participate (over $10,000 total).[15]

For in-home caregivers, you will also be required to pay Social Security, Medicare and federal unemployment taxes. If your employer offers flexible spending accounts, be sure

---

14. Ann Douglas, *The Unofficial Guide to Childcare* (Macmillan General Reference, 1998).

15. Ibid.

to take advantage of them. Depending upon your employer, you can put up to $5,000 away pre-tax for child-care. Be careful to accurately determine your estimated child care expenses. If you estimate the expenses at $4,500, but you only spend $4,000, you will lose $500.

Many women who work part time need only part-time childcare. If this is your goal, you should be aware that many day cares and nanny's charge the full-time rate for infants in cribs regardless of the time spent at the day care or with nannies. Many day cares and nannies assume that any crib could be taken up by a full-time infant, so they require you to pay for the lost income. In addition, many states that license day cares and nannies rightfully limit the number of infants that can be watched by one adult.

In the table below, an average cost was not calculated for part-time child care because there was a large difference between the hours worked by these part-timers.

| **Study Participants' Child Care Costs** | | |
|---|---|---|
| **Full-time working moms using** | **Cost Range (per week)** | **Average (per week)** |
| Day Care 62% of the Time | $107–$210 | $148 |
| Family Members 19% of the Time | $0–$200 | $67 |
| Nannies 13% of the Time | $300–$370 | $338 |
| Work Opposite Hours as Spouse 6% | Costs Nothing | — |
| **Part-time working moms using** | **Cost Range (per week)** | **Average (per week)** |
| Day care 45% of the Time | $50–$170 | — |
| Family Members 22% of the Time | $0–$45 | — |
| Nannies 11% of the Time | $265–$400 | — |
| Work Opposite Hours as Spouse 11% | Costs Nothing | — |
| Can Work and Watch Child 11% | Costs Nothing | — |

Seventy-two percent of the family members who are watching these children do it for free. If a family member is watching your children, unless they are extremely wealthy, they should be paid something. Most mothers would rather leave their children with family members, rather than with non-family. Family members are more likely to know your values and will be more able to instill those values. If you are lucky enough to have a family member who is enthusiastic about watching your children, pay them accordingly. If you can afford it, pay them up to the acceptable hourly wages for untrained nannies.

Ninety-five percent of the working mothers in the study are happy with their child care.

### Other Costs

The United States Department of Agriculture estimates that children born in 1997 will cost parents $353,130 (excluding college tuition) through age seventeen. However, families that plan to have only one child should expect to pay $437,881. In addition, high-income families spend about $12,000 per child during the first year. The $12,000 includes child care (but not the expensive child care associated with two parents working full time). The book *Baby Bargains* by Denise and Alan Fields[16] is a great place to learn how to identify less expensive quality baby products. It explains the baby gadgets that are necessities, those that are luxuries, and those that are a ridiculous waste of money. The cost of a four-year in-state college beginning in 2017 is expected to average $157,000.

Do not forget to have life insurance on both parents. Life insurance on a stay-at-home parent is just as important as on a working parent. If the stay-at-home parent dies, additional family costs would include a housekeeping

---

16. Denise and Alan Fields, *Baby Bargains* (Boulder, CO: Windsor Peak Press, 1997).

service, a laundry service, and child care. In addition, the remaining parent would have to function as two parents and would need to cut back on hours worked. The life insurance offered through work is often more costly, and the amount that one can purchase is limited. Review the life insurance that is available to you outside your employer. All it takes is a phone call to an insurance broker, a few health questions, and a nurse visiting your house for a blood and urine sample. It's worth it for the piece of mind you'll get.

## BUYING FRENZY & EVIL CREDIT CARDS

Consumer debt is at a record high. According to chief economist Mark Zandi, the liabilities owed by the average household doubled over the last twenty years from $20,000 to near $40,000.[17] However, the Census Bureau reports that the national median household income in 1998 was only $37,779. Therefore, the average family has a total debt in excess of their annual income.

Mark Zandi also found that the personal savings rate, which was at 8% in the 1970s and early 1980s, recently turned negative.[18] People have switched from saving their money to tapping into their savings and spending it.

Hyper-spending, increased household debt, and reduced savings has significantly increased the number of bankruptcies. The American Bankruptcy Institute found that bankruptcies were up 19.1% nationally in 1997. One in every seventy households in the U.S. filed for bankruptcy last year.

There are too many people today who are trying to compete with the Joneses and are spending money that

---

17. Mark Zandi, "Household Lending from Here to 2020," *Journal of Lending & Credit Risk Management* (September 1999). Mark Zandi is the chief economist and co-founder of RFA/Dismal Sciences, Inc. RFA stands for Regional Financial Associates. They are a national economic consulting firm located in Pennsylvania.

18. Ibid.

they do not have. Do not make purchases with a credit card, unless you have the cash in the bank to pay for it. Americans are "we have to have it now" consumers. Do you really need to furnish every room in your house the first year you move in? Our parents raised us with much less, and we didn't feel shortchanged. In fact, as a child, I remember our favorite room to play in was the living room, which for a time was empty of any furniture.

Lenders make it very tempting to use their credit cards. Too many people receive unsolicited credit cards in the mail and then use them. You do not need more than two credit cards.

Store credit cards are also unnecessary. I do not know of any store that only accepts their own store's cards anymore. Their fees and late payment penalties are generally much higher than traditional credit cards. Two general credit cards, checks, an ATM card, and a photo ID are all you really need. Throw out those other cards and do not accumulate any more.

If you do make purchases with credit cards, fully pay off those balances every month. Never make the minimum suggested payment. If you only make the minimum monthly payment, you will be paying for a very long time, and you will be paying a lot of interest.

People have gotten themselves so far in debt that they are refinancing their homes to consolidate all of their credit card bills. The lending companies' advertisements generally state something to the effect that "we can reduce your monthly payments, sometimes in half." What the commercials do not tell you is that you will be paying for an additional twenty years, and that it's going to add tens of thousands of dollars in additional interest. Of course if you are in debt up to your ears, refinancing or consolidating may be in your best interest. Be sure to do the math and cut up those credit cards.

Many banks automatically supply customers with debit cards. These cards allow bank customers to take cash directly out of the ATM machines and to make purchases at stores. They often have credit card logos on them, such as Visa or MasterCard; however, using a debit card does not automatically provide the protection that a credit card provides. For example, if you notice fraudulent purchases on your credit card and you notify the card company within sixty days, the most you will be out is $50. The federal protection for debit cards is much less. With debit cards, you have two days to limit your possible loss to $50. Otherwise, your potential loss goes up to $500 for two to sixty days, and beyond that it could be your bank balance plus your overdraft line. Some banks have voluntarily upped their protection to that of credit cards. However, it's voluntary and they can rescind it at any time.[19] If your bank offers you a debit card, turn it down for a normal ATM card that does not allow for purchases.

If you make purchases on the Internet, have one credit card with a limited balance dedicated to such on-line purchases. Many Internet retailers guarantee the security of your credit card information. However, if asked point blank if the information could be stolen or misused, they will tell you there is always the potential. They are always working to outmaneuver the latest hacker strategies. But as we all know, hackers sometimes beat them.

In addition, Internet companies are still working out the kinks in many of their systems. I recently tried to make an on-line purchase from a large on-line toy retailer. They made all types of guarantees against credit card misuse and had even received national recognition for their credit card procedures. After selecting the toys I wanted to purchase and entering my credit card information, the system came back and said my card had been denied. I then entered

---

19. Nancy Lloyd, *Simple Money Solutions* (Times Books, 2000).

another card and once again was told it had been denied. I then reentered the first card and was denied for a third time. I called my credit card companies and found out that the orders had not been denied, and that the retailer had actually put the orders through to my credit cards. The toy retailer later told me they had no record of those three orders because there was a human error the evening I placed my orders. They had taken the system down that day to load some updates and someone had forgotten to take the part of the system related to charging credit cards off line.

In the book *The Millionaire Next Door,* Thomas Stanley and William Danko studied individuals who accumulated wealth. They found that the average millionaires have very modest spending habits. They concluded that it's the under-accumulators who are engaged in hyper-consumption. The moral of their book is to simplify your life, and you will be happier for it.

For additional information on family financial planning, read *Love, Marriage, and Money* by Alan Lavine and Gall Liberman and *Simple Money Solutions* by Nancy Lloyd.

# Home Office Resources

A home office takes up space in your home that could be used for other purposes. Depending upon your needs, home office space could be an entire room dedicated to your business or a corner of a room.

I need my home office to be a separate room not used for anything else. There is always plenty of work to do for my job. If I had to pass my desk during the evening or on weekends, I would start thinking about the pile of work on my desk. I do not want to do that. My time off is time with my family (except for emergency work projects). I have enough trouble separating myself from work.

You should not be able to hear sounds from other parts of the house when you are working in your home office. I would never get any work done during the day if I could hear my daughter laughing or crying. It would be distracting. In addition, hearing home noises (such as a baby crying) in the background while talking on the phone is very unprofessional and distracting to whomever you are talking to.

To be honest, my dogs do sit under my desk during the day while I am working. They like to bark when they hear the FedEx man ring the doorbell. Luckily, this has happened only once over the last few years while I've been on the phone.

I know a woman with a young baby who is attempting a home office with no outside caregiver. When she's speaking on the phone and her baby is crying, I find it unprofessional and distracting. If you work for a company in a professional position and you attempt to do this, you will end up shortchanging the baby and your work. If you work for yourself, you can make up your own rules. You can decide that you are willing to lose sales to customers who do not want to hear a baby in the background.

Depending upon what I am purchasing, I do make purchases from women who are working while they watch their children. For example, there is a photographer in the area that takes wonderful pictures of children. She works part time and her children are playing in a corner of her studio (in her house) during all of her shoots. She doesn't create a demanding schedule for herself. When she does have customers, her children can play by themselves for an hour. I do not find this offensive.

Once children get a little older and they know their parents are working somewhere in the house, they can either find you and distract you, or they can make themselves upset because they want to see you and they are not allowed. When my daughter turned one, she began to get upset every time I would leave her to go back up to work after a break. I had to start sneaking around when I went downstairs for a cup of tea. Fortunately, that was a quick phase. Now when I get a snack, I can play a quick game of Ring Around the Rosy before I head back up, and I don't have to worry about a scene when I leave.

On the other hand, I have several friends who leave out the front door in the morning, as if they are going to work. They then sneak back into the house via the back door and go directly to their offices. I do not expect to have to do this in the future, but neither did they. My sister-in-law was one of those who snuck back in every day. She was often discovered because her office was in the basement, and there wasn't a bathroom on that floor.

If you are thinking of moving or redesigning your home, keep in mind the space and positioning of rooms that you will need if you someday have a home office. How much space will you require? I know my sister-in-law wishes she had designed a bathroom in their basement. Think about what you may need based upon what type of work you expect to be doing. Will you need a desk, a filing cabinet, a copier, a fax, bookshelves, telephone line connection, Internet connection, and so forth? Will your office need to be close to an exterior door because customers will be coming to your home?

Here are some cost estimates for home office equipment. Evaluate what you need versus what you want. A phone can range from $20 to $200. Computers range from $900 to $5,000. A good office chair will cost $200. Of course, a spare kitchen chair can always do in a pinch. Black-and-white printers range from $250 to $900. A good laser jet printer that prints eight pages per minute with 600 x 600 dpi (dots per inch) and a 100-sheet input bin will cost approximately $500 and will more than meet the demands of most home offices. A good plain paper fax will cost $250. If you plan to receive many faxes or if you need the faxes that you receive to look professional and last for years, purchase a plain paper fax over a thermal fax. If you do a lot of photocopying, you may want to invest in a copier. I make a lot of copies, so I invested in a copier with an automatic document feeder for $1,000. It does not collate or staple, but it meets my needs. If you do not need the automatic document feeder, you can find good copiers for under $500. When I first started out with a home office, I used my fax machine to make copies. The quality was so-so, but the price was right (free, since I already owned the fax machine). Keep in mind that the printer cartridges, fax cartridges, and photocopier cartridges and drums can be very expensive ($35 to $250 each).

Depending upon your field, an extra phone line dedicated to your home office endeavors may be essential. First, not everyone believes that individuals working from home can do as good of a job as individuals working in an office setting. By having a dedicated line installed, there may be nothing to give your home office away. What they don't know won't hurt them. Second, people today work around the clock. I receive a lot of calls from the West Coast and from individuals working late at night expecting to reach my voice mail. It's not unusual for me to receive business calls at 9:30 P.M. Eastern Time. If you do not want your after-hours personal life interrupted by picking up the phone only to find out that it is work related, install a line dedicated to your business. When I know the business line has rung after hours, I generally will check the message that evening, but at a convenient time for me. Third, for expense/tax purposes a separately billed dedicated line is much easier to account for. When calling to have the line installed and set up, it is often less expensive to have it set up as an extra home phone line. If you tell the phone company that it is work related, they often boost the cost.

When first starting out in a home office, determine what your minimum requirements are and what your budget is. If you can spend more on a printer or copier (or anything else that will make your life easier), do it. Investing in a home office is just like investing in your career. In addition, if you purchase equipment that meets your needs today, and you do not plan for what your future needs will be, you may quickly outgrow your equipment. If you are employed, hopefully your employer will pick up the tab for most of your home office needs.

# Fertility & Child Rearing (resources of eggs & energy)

## FACTORS IMPACTING WHEN WOMEN HAVE CHILDREN

Before my daughter was conceived, whenever my husband and I were asked when we would have children, our typical response was, "Maybe in two to three years." We gave this response for eight years. No matter what point in time we were asked, we truly believed we would have children in that time frame. The target continued to move because we wanted to be a little more financially secure, and I realized that the majority of my movement up the corporate ladder would have to take place before I had children. I knew once children arrived, they would be my top priority, and I would no longer regularly work evenings and weekends.

Then there was a surprise pregnancy, and our daughter was born when I was thirty. Had that wonderful surprise not occurred, realistically, we probably would have waited until I was thirty-five years old. Looking back, we couldn't have had her at a better time for us, and we are very glad she came when she did.

A major challenge facing today's professional women is how to obtain the education, certification, licensing, and optimal position before having children. Advances in contraception and in fertility allow women to dictate (within parameters) when they will have children. This provides women with a wider time frame in which to reach their goals. But even with scientific advances, women can only put off childbearing for so many years.

The study participants who planned to have children but did not yet have any were asked, "Why haven't you had any children?" Their answers were as follows:

- 53% said they were waiting until they got married,
- 15% until they were more financially secure,
- 8% until they were further along in their career,
- 7% were waiting until they were older, and
- 17% for various other reasons.

It's interesting to note that in this group of people twenty-eight to thirty-five years old that "waiting for marriage" was the number one reason for postponing children. Several of these women stated that they still had not met Mister Right, but they were keeping an open mind.

The women who planned to have children but did not have any expected, on average, to begin having them in 3.1 years.

Of the study participants who were already mothers,

- 50% didn't postpone having children once they were married;
- 15% postponed having children until they were further along in their careers;
- 13% postponed having children until they obtained additional degrees or certification;

- 5% postponed for financial reasons;
- 5% postponed to spend time with spouse (once married) before children came into the picture; and
- 12% postponed for various other reasons (including difficulty getting pregnant, for husband to obtain additional degree, and emotional growth).

## WOMEN IN THEIR TWENTIES

Physically, the best time for women to become pregnant and deliver healthy babies is while they are in their late teens and early twenties. However, a twenty-two-year-old college graduate probably only has one year of work experience, still isn't sure where she wants her career to go, and hasn't had time to obtain the licenses, certifications, or graduate degrees that will enable her to move up the ladder. In addition, most twenty-two-year-old women will not have been with their employers long enough to negotiate for a family-friendly position (part time, flextime, or working from a home office). A few entry-level positions start employees out in home offices. Generally, these are sales positions.

If you are interested in obtaining all of the further education, certification, licensing, and experience needed for you to be eligible for a specific position (career), you may want to look into postponing children. If you follow a low-risk contraception method faithfully, you shouldn't have any surprises, and you should be able to have some time to reach the goals that you have scheduled for yourself. If you are interested in contraception, speak with your health care provider about the risks associated with the various methods. Depending upon your religion, you may also want to speak with your religious leader.

If you have your children in your early twenties, you are less likely to have achieved a family-friendly position that provides a good income. However, if being a young parent and having lots of energy while your children are young is very important to you, then being a parent while in your twenties may be the best decision for you.

If you want to get pregnant, there are home tests that will increase your chance of conception. The new ovulation predictor tests detect the LH (luteinizing hormone) surge in urine that occurs just before ovulation. Women are most likely to become pregnant within thirty-six hours of detecting the LH surge. But do not use the ovulation predicator tests for contraception. Sperm can survive up to three days, but these tests only predict that ovulation will occur within thirty-six hours. If you fool around on Day 1, have a test that shows the LH surge on Day 2, and ovulate on Day 3, sperm may still be around to fertilize that egg.

These test kits are expensive, and if you are in your twenties, probably unnecessary. A woman's health care provider should be able to educate you about the signs of ovulation.

For those of you wondering whether you are too old and tired to have children, consider that my daughter was born when I was thirty. My husband and I didn't have the energy we had when we were twenty; however, after she was born, energy appeared from nowhere. Just looking at your precious child will provide you with the inspiration needed to take that twelfth trip up the stairs to change a diaper or to sit on the floor and play games for hours. The energy appears, no matter how old you are.

## WOMEN OVER THIRTY-FIVE

For those of you who want to postpone starting a family until your career has moved along and you are more financially stable, you should know the facts concerning fertility and pregnancy problems that increase with age. This information is not being provided to scare you. It's being provided so that you can make an informed decision. Most women are not acquainted with these figures until there is a problem.

First trimester spontaneous miscarriages increase progressively with each year over age thirty. The risk is 10% for women younger than thirty, 18 to 20% for women between the ages of thirty-five and thirty-nine, 30 to 45% for women over forty, and more than 53% for women over forty-five.[20]

The risk of having a child with Down's syndrome is 1 in 1,667 at twenty years old, 1 in 952 at thirty years old, 1 in 378 at thirty-five years old, 1 in 106 at forty years old, and 1 in 30 at age forty-five.[21] Today's medical advances allow perspective parents to learn before their child is born whether he has Down's syndrome. This information should be used to best prepare and learn about Down's syndrome, what to expect, and how to cope. There aren't any tests that can completely guarantee that a child will be born without birth defects.

In addition, the older a woman is, the more time there is for her to develop chronic health problems that increase her risk of developing other problems during pregnancy (such as hypertension and diabetes). However, the biggest obstacle faced by women over thirty-five years of age is becoming pregnant at all because of decreased fertility.

| Chances of Getting Pregnant per Cycle[22] | |
|---|---|
| **Age** | **Chance** |
| 15 | 40–50% |
| 25 | 30–35% |
| 35 | 15–20% |
| 45 | 3–5% |

20. Howard I. Shapiro, M.D., *The Pregnancy Book for Today's Woman* (New York: Harper Collins, 1993), 40–41.

21. Ibid, 403.

22. *Dr. Richard Marr's Fertility Book* (Dell, 1997).

Keep in mind, medical science has significantly increased an older woman's chance of becoming pregnant and delivering a healthy child. The number of women over thirty-five who are having babies is increasing dramatically. If you are thinking of waiting to become pregnant, speak with your health care provider.

If you become pregnant later in life, you won't be alone. More and more women are giving birth to children later in life. The list of women who were over forty when they became pregnant includes Annette Bening, Kim Basinger, Emma Thompson, Tanya Tucker, and Christiane Amanpour (from CNN).

Unlike men who can produce sperm throughout their lives, women are born with a limited number of eggs. Once those eggs are gone, they are gone. Again, medical science can intervene by using someone else's eggs. However, most women would choose conception earlier in life over that alternative because of the expense and pain, and the emotional and legal issues involved.

Adoption is another alternative. On the average, U.S. adoptions cost $15,000 and generally take twelve to eighteen months. International adoptions range from $13,000 to $20,000 per child, depending upon the country. The average price in China is $10,000 to $15,000, depending on whether one or both parents make the trip. If you contemplate adoption, you have a lot of research ahead of you.

## Spacing Between Children

The *New England Journal of Medicine* published a study in February 1999 that concluded that infants born about two and a half years after a sibling (conceived twenty-one months after the birth of a sibling) were least likely to be premature or unusually small. Undesirable outcomes were 30 to 40% higher for children born fifteen months after a sibling (conceived six months after the birth of a sibling). The study also found that a sibling was twice as likely to be born prematurely if there was ten years between the children.

Even though this study received a lot of attention, it does not mean much to the average person. Very few mothers attempt to conceive while their child is only six months old. The close pregnancies that do occur may be due to the fact that some mothers do not realize that they can get pregnant while they are breast-feeding. Breast-feeding (without supplementing with formula or food and with nighttime feedings) does reduce a woman's chance of becoming pregnant during the first few months of her child's life. However, this is not a foolproof method. If you are breast-feeding your child and you do not want to conceive, take precautions.

The conclusion that children born ten years after a sibling have more undesirable outcomes is common sense based on the fact that the mother is ten years older with the second child. Her chances of having a miscarriage or a child with Down's syndrome has increased due to her age.

Children are very resilient no matter how close or spread out their births are. They bring so much to the table that it's probably not worth worrying about how close or far apart they are.

# Review Your Goals in Light of the Resources That They Would Require

Earlier, I listed the goals for my expectation of "providing the best family life for my future children." I have repeated these goals below:

1. Working to maintain a strong family relationship
2. Either my husband or me achieving a career that

would enable one of us to stay at home with the children, or a combination of both careers and some flexibility (part time, flextime, home office) that would enable us to raise our children

3. Spending quality time with the children
   a. Instilling within the children the importance of becoming productive individuals, then creating the drive for them to achieve it
   b. Teaching our morals and values to our children and setting a good example in practice
   c. Introducing the children to social settings where they can learn to interact with others and providing an ear when tough lessons are learned
   d. Involving the children in family discussions where we rely on each other and our extended family (e.g. grandma picking a child up from school when the child is sick)
   e. Setting a good example of being there for the family and extended family when needed
   f. Taking time out of every day to teach the children and make it an enjoyable experience

4. Taking time to enjoy life with the children on a daily basis

5. Earning more than enough to provide a nice home, necessities, college tuition, some extravagances, and have a nice nest egg left over to do what we want when we retire.

The resources required to meet these goals would be

1. time (attention),
2. time (attention) and money,
3. time (attention),
4. time (attention), and
5. money.

Do you see the pattern? Time (attention) is the number one resource that is going to be stretched by these goals. Money (income) will also have a significant impact on whether these goals are achieved.

According to Cindi Swernofsky (education coordinator at the Child Care Council of Nassau County), 70% of women nationwide are working for economic reasons.[23] Therefore, many working women work because they require the resource of money.

As stated earlier in this book, the following reasons are given by mothers for working:

- 44% work for the money.
- 31% work because they like what they do for a living.
- 10% work because their career provides something that they need (power, self-fulfillment, and so forth).
- 15% work for various other reasons, including maintaining skills, the benefits, because they like to work, or because they like their job and it wasn't guaranteed to be there if they took off time from work.

The difference between the percentage of women, nationally, who are working for economic reasons and the percentage of women in this study who work is partially due to the fact that all of the study participants were educated women. Educated women are more likely to earn more. They are also more likely to marry educated men. The higher a man's education, the more likely he'll be earning more money. The more money a husband earns, the less pressure on the wife to work for economic reasons.

---

23. Elio Evangelista, "Tutor Time Centers Flourish on Island / Demand Created 3 New Sites Last Year," *Newsday* (19 March 1999): Business Section: A54.

Your list of goals and expectations will be very long. Make sure that the resources required to meet all of your goals are available. If there are not enough resources to meet your goals, you will need to eliminate or make compromises. Generally, goals related to your top expectations will remain, and goals related to expectations lower on your list may be postponed or eliminated altogether.

# CHAPTER 5

# Other Items
# Impacting Your Goals

Now that you have reevaluated your goals based upon a limited amount of resources, you will need to reevaluate your goals based upon a few other items.

## Chosen Profession

The profession that you have chosen for yourself may not be conducive to meeting your goals. Review your goals in light of your chosen profession. For example, one of your goals may be to live out in the country, but your chosen profession may require you to be physically in the city everyday. Look for compromises such as various career alternatives, postponing the move to the country until later in life, or eliminating that goal for the time being.

If your goal is to eventually work from home on a regular basis, evaluate that goal in light of the profession that you have chosen. For example, if you have chosen nursing and also plan to work from home in your future, identify the alternatives available for working in this profession from home. If you cannot identify any, you may need to reevaluate your goals.

Very specialized professions are generally not advertised, nor are they discussed in career planning literature. Therefore, these specialties are not known to most. The best way to learn about such niche occupations is by speaking with others in your field and keeping your eyes open. Specialty professions often earn more than their counterparts in the more recognized general professions. If you recognize a need for a specialist in your field, analyze the opportunity and market for such specialists.

While researching, planning, and analyzing your profession, do not lose site of the fact that the most important factor in choosing a profession is to make sure it's something you love to do.

## RESEARCH THE OUTLOOK FOR YOUR PROFESSION

Read books, articles, and Web pages that address where your profession is heading. For example, if you are planning to be a COBOL programmer, you should be aware that most new programs are no longer written in COBOL. The high demand for COBOL programmers in 1999 was merely due to the need to rewrite old COBOL programs to avoid the Y2K glitch. By 2003, the demand for COBOL programmers is expected to have dropped significantly.

Many Web sites provide the outlook for occupations. Here are three free places to visit on the Web:

- www.bls.gov is the home page for the Bureau of Labor Statistics. Click on "Occupational Outlook Handbook." Most college graduates will find their profession under the occupational cluster of "Professional and Technical Occupations." It provides information about the nature of the work, working conditions, employment, training, other qualifications, advancement, job outlook, earnings, related occupations, and sources of additional information for more than 250 occupations.
- www.careers.wsj.com is from the publishers of *The Wall Street Journal.* It provides the salaries and profiles for many occupations.
- www.acinet.org is from America's Career InfoNet: Wages and Trends.

In addition, contact several individuals who are already in your chosen field and ask them for their outlook on the profession. Most people are very willing to answer questions about their career. A good place to start is with your college's alumni. A school's alumni directory (whether in the form of a book, CD, or on-line) is "the source" for locating alumni employed in your profession. Most people, if they were to receive a call from a student who is attending (or attended) their alma mater, would be very willing to answer career-related questions. If they are not willing to speak with you, you have lost nothing. If they are willing to speak with you, you will gain an abundance of knowledge. Obtain several individuals' opinions. Compare their outlooks. Analyze the differences and similarities between them.

No one is going to spoon-feed you what your profession is like in the real world. It's your responsibility to find out what your profession entails besides the technical aspects that your education is preparing you for. Questions to ask individuals in your chosen profession include:

- What has their overall experience been?
- Were they surprised by anything?
- Did their career meet their expectations?
- Would they change anything?
- What is a reasonable compensation in this profession at the entry level? What about five and ten years down the road?
- Where do you see the profession heading?
- What are the work hours expected from someone in this field?
- What are the internal politics in this profession?

Many people would change their profession, if they had it to do all over again. In fact, 34% of the study participants would change their major in college if they could do it over again. This emphasizes the need for more career research and planning.

For example, many public accountants have made significant compromises in their lives to pass the CPA exam and to work long hours. Yet, many accountants are often surprised to find out that individuals who went into what they deemed to be less demanding majors in college are now earning more than they are, while working fewer hours. Do your research ahead of time, so you aren't regretting your career decisions later on.

New entries into the nursing profession are often surprised by the repetitive nature of their daily duties. Their duties often include going from room to room and signing their name over and over again on each patient's chart. Additionally, nurses tend to spend a lot of time on their feet and are generally physically and mentally exhausted by the time their shifts end. Learn the nuances of your profession prior to entering the workforce. There may be sub-disciplines within a profession that you would find more appealing.

There are often regional differences between professions. For example, associate lawyers in New York firms are more likely to be put through the grindstone and become burned out than associate lawyers in other regions. Of course, the New York lawyers are compensated for their sacrifices by being paid up to twice as much as lawyers in other regions of the country.

Your profession's future will be essential to your achieving your goals.

## ENTREPRENEURS

The good news for would-be female entrepreneurs is that women are starting and succeeding at owning their own businesses in record numbers. The bad news is that the U.S. Small Business Administration has found that 75 to 80% of all new businesses fail within their first five years.

If you decide to start your own business, be prepared for all the paperwork required by the city, state, and federal agencies. You will need to be a doer who can get things accomplished in order to survive.

Several organizations and programs are dedicated to guiding women through the start-up process. Take advantage of them. Many of them have helped make it easier for women to obtain loans.

If you plan to eventually break out on your own and become an entrepreneur, give it your all and back it up with the necessary research and planning. There is a plethora of books written about how to choose a business and how to start a new business. Read them.

## WILL YOUR CHOSEN PROFESSION PROVIDE THE INCOME TO MEET YOUR MONETARY GOALS?

Back in the section of this book titled "What Are Others in Your Profession Earning?" beginning on page 50, you learned how to determine what others in your profession are earning. Evaluate what you should be earning five, ten, fifteen, or more years from now. Will this income meet your monetary goals during various stages of your life?

If your goals include achieving a large future salary, but you have picked an occupation that does not have a large income potential, you will need to reevaluate. What is more important to you, the reasons behind why you would like the larger income, or the reasons behind your career choice?

Assume your goals were to make a lot of money and to be a social worker. These two goals are generally not compatible. Female social workers are paid on average $30,000 a year. Therefore, the profession may not be conducive to meeting your monetary goal. Under this scenario, you have three basic options.

First, you can revise your monetary goal down. If the profession you have chosen will not provide the income to meet your goals, but remaining in this profession is very important to you, evaluate changing your monetary goals. For example, you may decide that staying in your current profession is more important to you than moving into that large house, buying that new couch, or having a huge nest egg for retirement. Most social workers do not choose their profession for the pay.

Your second option is to look for specialties within your field that pay more. Social workers in private practice earn $57,000 on average.

Your third option is to reevaluate the profession that you have chosen. Did you choose this career because you wanted to help people and you are good at it? Evaluate other careers that would meet these needs while providing an income level more in line with your goals.

# Education

Education is the most essential component for obtaining fulfilling and lucrative positions. On the average, women with college degrees earn 2.5 times what women *without* high school diplomas earn.[24] Workers with four-year college degrees earn 1.5 times the average of what workers *with* high school diplomas earn.[25] Throughout this book, I have worked under the assumption that you are either striving to achieve an undergraduate degree or have achieved your undergraduate degree. If you do not follow through on obtaining an undergraduate degree, you are limiting yourself. Very few people find fulfilling jobs that pay reasonable salaries relying solely on high school diplomas. It *can* be done; however, most of those who made it without a college degree agree that it would have been easier with one. It's never too late to go back to school.

This section dedicated to education is broken down into four parts. First, how important is the name of your school and your grades in the real world? The second topic covers community colleges and junior colleges. If you have not or did not attend a community college, read this section anyway. It provides a good example of how to achieve your goals via alternate paths. The third covers issues related to graduate school. If you are not planning to attend graduate school, read this topic anyway — you may change your mind. The last topic discusses other types of education.

---

24. U.S. Department of Labor, Bureau of Statistics, "Highlights of Women's Earnings in 1998," report 928 (April 1999). Report 928 stated that "In 1998, women without high school diplomas had earnings that were 40% of those of female college graduates."

25. Recent census data shows workers with bachelor's degrees earned an average of $41,579 in 1997, compared with $27,005 for those who held only a high school diploma.

## How Important Are Your Grades & the Name of Your School in the Real World?

The name of your school and your grades are the most important factors in obtaining the best entry-level jobs in a profession. They are also the most important factors in being accepted into the best graduate schools. However, once you have been working a few years, the name of the school(s) you attended and your grades decrease in importance. They may get you in an employer's door, but they won't keep you there if you aren't doing a good job.

However, if the school you attended wasn't one of the premier schools, or your grades were only so-so, achieving the best first positions and getting into the best graduate schools will be more difficult. Attack obtaining your first job like it's a job unto itself. Chapter 7's section titled "Obtaining a New Job" will guide you through this process. Create great resumes and cover letters. Be prepared for interview questions. Research job openings. Apply for every position that meets your criteria. The more positions you apply for and the more interviews you have, the more job offers you will receive.

The key to moving up once you are employed in a profession is performance. Potential employers will look at what you have done in past positions and evaluate what you could do for them in the future. Experience, attitude, ambition, and credentials (licensing, certification, graduate degree) will all be important. However, the school you attended and the grades you received will generally have little impact on whether you are offered a position later in your career. There are very few exceptions to this rule.

The medical school that a doctor attends and the grades she earns will impact the positions that she is offered. However, think of your own doctors. Do you know which schools they attended and whether those schools are at the top or bottom for medical schools? Most people don't. There comes a point in time when even the medical schools that doctors attended are not as important as they had been earlier in the doctors' career. Just the fact that they are doctors and that they have worked ambitiously to create their practices is enough.

An "A" student from a prestigious school who hasn't done much with her career can end up in a lower position making less than a "C" student who attended night school at a local community college, if the "C" student's work performance has been very good. Just because someone excels in college does not mean they can hack it in the real world. And just because someone has trouble in college does not mean that they won't excel in the real world.

Thomas Edison, Henry Ford, Abraham Lincoln, and Mark Twain never finished grade school. Peter Jennings and Julia Roberts dropped out of high school. Candice Bergen, Walter Cronkite, Clint Eastwood, Harrison Ford, Ann Landers, and Steven Spielberg never finished college. Eugene O'Neil and John Steinbeck, who both won the Nobel Prize in literature, also never finished college. This list of people who made it without graduating with honors from a top-notch university emphasizes the fact that graduating with less than great grades from a mediocre college does not mean the end of what otherwise could be a great career. What all great achievers have in common is attitude and a dream.

You will find some career counselors who believe that obtaining the highest grades and SAT scores and enrolling at premier schools is the only way to make it to the top. They are generally wrong. Very few fields are that cutthroat. In most professions, you can still make it to the top without these things by taking a different route.

## COMMUNITY COLLEGES & JUNIOR COLLEGES

Over the last ten years, the academic community and employers have taken community colleges much more seriously. Many people who otherwise would not be attending college can now do so because of these local colleges. People attend these schools for various reasons, including:

- They find these schools are often less expensive;
- they may not have been accepted by any other schools;
- they were unsure what they wanted to do with their lives;
- these schools may be closer to their home; and
- these schools may offer more flexible schedules and evening courses.

I took two courses at the local community college one summer to ease my course load the following fall. People attend community colleges for various reasons.

If you are attending a college with the sole purpose of attaining an associate's degree (two-year degree), research whether there is a market for people with that degree. Generally, associate's degrees do not lead to great careers and large salaries. Look in the classifieds for positions for individuals holding associate's degrees in your field. Do not go into it with your eyes closed. What positions are obtainable with this degree? What salary can you expect? How many of these positions exist? The best thing about associate's degrees is that with additional courses they can often turn into bachelor's degrees, which are much more marketable. There are a few career paths via associate's degrees that have a larger earnings potential and are marketable. One such area is in the field of computer programming. However, individuals who obtain additional degrees will substantially increase their opportunities.

If you are planning to attend a community college with the intention of eventually transferring the credits to another school, know the transfer policies of the school you wish to transfer to. Some schools limit the number of course or credit hours that you can transfer. Other schools will only accept courses from accredited schools. Still other schools will only accept the basic required courses outside your major. Most schools use a combination of these policies. Do not obtain your associate's degree with the assumption that all of your credits will transfer.

Too many people coming from community colleges are surprised to find out that only a small portion of their credits will transfer. Before I took my two summer courses at the local community college, I was required to obtain descriptions of what would be taught during the classes. Only when my school's administration found that the courses would be very similar to classes held at my school would they provide me with a statement stating they would accept these courses for credit transfer if I received a "B" or higher in them. Only after receiving this in writing did I enroll in these two courses.

If you plan to attend a community college, or have attended one already, do not be embarrassed by it. Obtaining a degree is an exceptional achievement, no matter what school it comes from. Be proud that you earned your degree. After you have been working for a little while, where your degree was earned will not be so important. If asked where you went to school, say it clearly. Do not look down or shrug your shoulders. Your body can give away the fact that you are not proud of your schooling. If you are not proud of it, you cannot expect others to be. Always be self-confident and proud of what you achieved. You'll go farther.

When you are just coming out of school, obtaining the better initial positions will be more difficult with a degree from a community college. You can overcome this by doing great work and moving up from one employer to another. You will probably have to make several more career jumps than someone coming from a prestigious school. For example, if you obtain a bachelor's degree in accounting from a community college, it's doubtful that one of the Big 5 firms will hire you. However, you can always start at a local accounting firm, earn your CPA, move on to a regional firm, and then make the jump to the Big 5. You are not stopped from making it to the top, you just have to take a different path to get there. Some people find that once they reach what they thought would be the pinnacle position, they no longer want the pressure and stress at the top. However, the climb up to the top is never in vain. The experience will substantially increase your options.

## GRADUATE SCHOOL

The impact a graduate degree (master's or doctorate) has on compensation is dependent upon the profession. Not all graduate degrees significantly increase compensation above what is made by individuals holding bachelor's degrees. For example, achieving a master's degree in journalism will earn the holder an increased salary of $4,000, on the average. On the other hand, a master's degree achieved in agricultural engineering can increase a salary by nearly $30,000.

People have different reasons for obtaining graduate degrees. There are several professions where you will not be able to get your foot in the door without a graduate degree. Other people achieve graduate degrees so they can move farther up the ladder more quickly. Still others do it for the money. But most people do it for a combination of these reasons.

## Cost

Attending graduate school is generally much more expensive than attending a four-year undergraduate program. The cost generally depends on the region where the school is located, whether it's a private school, what your field is, and your school's rank. A master's degree can easily cost twice as much as an undergraduate degree. A Ph.D. can cost five times as much as an undergraduate degree.

Your choices will significantly impact those costs. My undergraduate degree (tuition, room, and board) cost four times as much as my graduate degree (tuition only — I lived at home). The fact that I was paying my own way through graduate school greatly affected my graduate school decisions.

When comparing the cost of schools, do not compare one school's cost per credit hour with another school's cost per credit hour. There are many schools that charge more per credit hour, but require less credit hours to graduate. I've met several intelligent people who made the mistake of comparing cost per credit hour instead of total tuition.

I received a Master's of Taxation from Villanova Law's Graduate Tax Program for CPAs and attorneys. In my profession, I run into many individuals who have graduate tax degrees. I have met at least a dozen who told me that they chose to attend another school because Villanova's Graduate Tax Program was too expensive. They could not have done the math. When I was choosing schools, Villanova did have the highest cost per credit hour, but required the fewest credit hours. Overall, any cost differential was miniscule.

Graduate schools offering *similar degrees* often place a different emphasis on their curriculums, leading the professionals who obtain these degrees in different directions. For example, there are three graduate degrees offered by various colleges for tax specialists. There is the MBA

(Master's of Business Administration) with an emphasis in tax. To earn this degree, many fine universities require students to take a total of four tax courses and many business courses. The MS (Master's of Science) in tax is often taught from the view of a tax return preparer. The MT (Master's of Taxation) is often taught from the legal view of taxation. All are great degrees that add to an individual's earnings potential; however, each one is geared for individuals looking to specialize in different areas of taxation. If you are going to attend graduate school, pick the school and program that will meet your career aspirations, while staying within your financial boundaries.

### Time

In addition to the monetary sacrifice of attending graduate school, there is the time that it takes to attend graduate school. Again, it will depend upon which school you choose and your field. For example, an MBA degree generally takes two years. However, there are several schools that offer programs that can be completed in less than one year. On the other hand, a doctorate in English usually requires ten years of study and research. In addition, a school that requires fewer credit hours to graduate will not necessarily require less class time.

If you are thinking about taking time off from your career (or postponing entering the workforce) to attend graduate school full time, then go for it. Two years is just a blip on the screen and it shows great ambition. The two reasons to attend part time instead of full time are

- cost, and
- you have great satisfaction with your current position and are afraid that your position won't be there when you return.

The earlier you begin attending graduate school, the better (assuming you know the profession and degree that you want to obtain). The long-term benefits versus cost are much greater earlier in your career. In addition, attending graduate school is much easier prior to having children. Of course, it's never too late. Many women do not decide on a specialty until they have been in the workforce for several years.

### Compare the Expense (money and time) of Attending Graduate School with the Benefits

Assume that

- you are currently earning $40,000 a year;
- graduate school would cost $16,000 and would take two years of your time;
- the graduate degree would increase your salary by $15,000 a year to begin;
- you are twenty-five when you enter graduate school full time; and
- you expect to work full time from age twenty-seven through age sixty-three.

The cost of attending the graduate school is

| | |
|---|---|
| $80,000 | (two years of lost work revenue, assuming you attend full time) |
| + $16,000 | (tuition) |
| $96,000. | |

The benefit of a graduate degree over a nine-year period is $105,000. This is a $15,000 increase for seven years, including no increase for the two years you were in graduate school. This calculation does not take into account that average raises applied to the $15,000 pay increase would generally increase the pay difference earned under the two degrees every year.

The $96,000 cost would be made up within nine years under this scenario. After nine years (at the age of thirty-four), the increased salary would become pure reward. From age thirty-four to age sixty-three, the benefit from the advanced degree would be $450,000. This calculation assumes no raises, no additional leaps due to degree, and does not consider the time value of money and interest. The lifetime benefit from this degree would be more than $450,000.

Perform the same calculations for your own situation. Do the research and perform the calculation even if you are not planning to attend graduate school. You may change your mind.

If you obtain your graduate degree while working, you may have to change employers after receiving the graduate degree in order to obtain the pay increase. Not all employers see the advantage of hiring individuals with graduate degrees.

### OTHER TYPES OF EDUCATION

Other than obtaining degrees, all of us could use some improvement. It could be in the use of a word processor, spreadsheets, E-mail, research skills, finances, self-esteem, stress reduction, organization skills, anger management, communication skills, business writing, and so on.

Know your strengths and weaknesses. Learn the skills that would improve you as a professional in your field. If you have the time, take courses or read relevant articles and books on the subjects. But do not go crazy trying to do everything.

## Current Position

Staying with your current employer may not be conducive to meeting your goals. Reevaluate your current position in light of your goals.

When the study participants were asked what they would change if they had it to do all over again, 29% said they would change their career paths (specifically, the companies they worked for and the positions they went for). Professionals need to thoroughly review the positions they take and frequently evaluate whether to stay with their current employers.

## SWITCHING EMPLOYERS IS NOW ACCEPTABLE

In today's environment, it's unusual to stick with the same employer for the long term. Job applicants with multiple employers are no longer at a disadvantage. It's just part of doing business. According to the academic consulting firm Universum, 80% of the 2,221 U.S. MBA students surveyed planned to stay at their first jobs less than five years. They also found that the number one quality these students wanted in their ideal employer was "a good reference for my future career."[26]

As companies have become larger and more impersonal, they no longer have the same employee loyalty. In return, employees no longer feel obligated to stay with companies when better opportunities arise. Of course, there are companies that are loyal to their employees, and most individuals have trouble saying good-bye to good employers. However, everyone should look out for number one in the end.

My brother-in-law worked for a nationally recognized company that recently called in his whole department (sixty employees) and told them they had two hours to pack up because they were outsourcing the whole department. The news came as a shock to everyone. Thankfully, between the great economy and his professional reputation, he had several offers from other companies within a

---

26. Shelly Branch, "MBA's: What They Really Want," *Fortune* 137(5) (16 March 1998): 167.

week. The moral of this story is that no matter how comfortable you feel in your position with your employer,
there is always the chance that you could be let go.
Companies will do whatever they believe is in their best
interest. You need to follow their lead and do whatever is in
your best interest. It's not easy leaving a company you
enjoyed working for or asking for a raise, but there are
times when it is necessary.

## *IF YOU ARE UNDERPAID*

From conducting the research described in the section
"What are others in your profession earning," back on page
50, you should already have a good idea about what others
in your position are earning. If your current employer is
not paying you what you believe you could be earning elsewhere, it's probably time to look into it. However, don't go
off half-cocked. Have all of your ducks in a row before
walking into your boss's office.

Never get involved in workplace gossip, especially when
it comes to salaries. It's unprofessional. Stay above it. It does
not matter whether your peers are underpaid. Take the bull
by the horns and do what's best for you. Many companies
pay employees performing similar tasks significantly different salaries. It's all a matter of which employees know what
they are worth and which employees use their best negotiating skills. However, even if you know you are worth more
than you are being paid and you are willing to negotiate, if
your employer thinks you are a gossip, you won't have a
chance of earning on the higher end. Businesses do not
want everyone to know that others in the same position are
making more.

Once you have the figures for what the average employees in your profession are earning, it's time to take the next
step. Clean up your resume, brush up on your interviewing

skills, and apply with several potential employers. It's important to do this every few years, whether you are planning to leave your current employer or not. The actual offers that you receive will be the best source of information about what others believe you are worth.

Armed with this information, it's time to go back to your employer and start discussing a raise. It does not have to be from the perspective that "If I don't get a raise, I'll leave" (unless of course, you are really thinking about taking the other position). Merely have an honest discussion with your employer laying out,

- "Here is what I earn,"
- "Here is what others earn on average in my profession" (provide your employer with supporting documentation from your research), and
- "Here is what I have been offered as a starting salary to join other companies."

Do not forget to add, "I put everything into my work here, all of my evaluations have been good, I enjoy what I do, and I enjoy working here." Then it's time to throw it back to them and have them respond to the *fact* that you are being underpaid. It will be tough for them to argue with such a well laid out case.

The response that many companies will come back with is that they just cannot afford to meet that salary, but they'll meet you somewhere between the two. Then it's up to you. You can negotiate further, accept their offer, or decline their offer. Realize that they may be telling you the truth that they cannot afford to pay you more. However, evaluate the option of staying versus meeting your monetary goals. Having pity for your company is not always the best reason to stay. Morally it feels good, but realize that many of the women I interviewed for this study wished they had left a previous employer earlier than they had.

Employees who stay with companies over a period of time need to evaluate what they are being paid every few years. Often, raises do not keep up with what the market is willing to pay. It's part of doing business. For example, I have a friend who owns a business with over eighty employees. He's just trying to earn an honest living. Many of his employees perform the same duties and are equally important to his company; however, there is a wide discrepancy between some of their salaries. This is due to the fact that some employees know what they are worth and speak with him about it, while other employees just accept their annual raises and are naive about what they could make elsewhere. If you do not know what you are worth, or you do not speak up, you are going to make less than you otherwise could. But do not go to your boss every year threatening to leave if your latest offer is not matched. It's unrealistic to expect an employer to match top market price every year.

I interviewed several women who were in charge of human resource departments. The companies they worked for were similar in size and located in the same region. They had similar credentials, backgrounds, and responsibilities. However, there was a $30,000 discrepancy between their salaries. It's everyone's responsibility to know what they are worth.

Of course, there are always going to be individuals who believe they should be paid more even though they are not worth it. These people generally never realize that their personality, attitude, or aptitude is holding them back.

The skills and attributes that are necessary when asking for a salary increase are just as important when you are asking for anything else that is important to you (whether it's a promotion, or the right to work from a home office, or to work flextime or part time). If you do not have the backbone to ask for something, it's unlikely that you will ever achieve it. Whatever you are asking for, do your homework, be prepared, and be ready to negotiate. Evaluate what the worst thing that can happen is if your request is denied. Generally, the worst thing that can happen is that you will have to hear the word "no."

## OVERCOMING ENTRY-LEVEL BIAS

Another obstacle you may need to overcome is an employer's unconscious "entry-level bias."

- If you are still with the same employer that hired you straight out of college,
- if over the years, your company has established a pattern of hiring individuals from outside the company for positions that you believed you were ready for, and
- if these individuals have the same (or less) experience than you,

then your employer may be having trouble viewing you as you currently are (with the experience, knowledge, and self-esteem you gained while working for them).

When we are all starting out, we make mistakes, have lower self-esteem, and are less assertive. We are not the same people we grow to be over time. Many first employers unintentionally hang on to their first impressions. It is much harder to overcome these first impressions than to start afresh with a new employer where you have a blank slate, nothing to overcome, and you can just dazzle them by doing a great job.

Once someone holds a bad impression of you, it's tough to overcome. Sometimes it's necessary to break with the individuals who hold these impressions in order to reach your full potential. The jump from high school to college can be very similar to moving between jobs. For example, a high school senior may have a reputation for not being on the ball. However, that student may simply have not worked to achieve in high school. When he goes off to college, he is given a fresh slate. He probably will know very few people on campus and can become a book-worm, if that is what he wants. When someone starts afresh with a new company, they are not held back by previous perceptions or stereotypes.

It's very difficult to overcome an unconscious bias held by an employer. One woman I interviewed worked as a book-keeper in an accounting firm for years while she obtained a B.S. in accounting at night. For years after she received her bachelor's degree, she was still being paid at a paraprofessional level. One of her responsibilities was to review the tax returns prepared by entry-level accountants fresh out of college who were being paid more than she was. She left the accounting firm that could not see their own bias and now works for a competitor at market price (twice her previous salary).

Not all companies have this unconscious entry-level bias. Many employers that hire recent college graduates do so with the foresight of the professionals that these new employees will become. That said, there are still many other common reasons to switch employers — the main one being that the biggest jumps in salary come from changing employers. Of course, if you are at a good company that is paying you fairly, then stay.

## WILL YOUR CURRENT POSITION MEET YOUR CAREER GOALS?

Evaluate whether your current position is leading you towards your career goals. If you have a goal of obtaining a specific position in your career, is staying in your current position going to help you obtain that future position?

Could you get there faster if you changed employers? It would be nice to have a crystal ball to tell us the future. But since there isn't such a thing, we need to rely on common sense and a little gut instinct when deciding what we need to do. Fear of change is not a good reason for staying in a position that is not going to get you to where you want to go. Too many women limit themselves because of fear.

Many women know what needs to be done, but put it off and never get to where they dream of going. Procrastination is a waste of time. The statement "I'll look into it tomorrow" often turns into never. Many women know what needs to be done. Yet, they put it off and never get to where they dream of going.

Generally, the worst thing that can possibly happen when you take a new job is that you will not like it. Being unhappy in a new position usually can be attributed to not conducting the necessary research before accepting the position. Keep in mind that it's tough to make significant advances without taking a few chances and making mistakes.

If you make a wrong decision, you'll learn from it and still be better off in the long run. Assume you change employers and the new one is worse than the old one. You will take from this life experience a better understanding of how to recognize companies like this. The next time you will perform more in-depth research on the companies you interview with. You will also ask them more direct and pointed questions that will increase your chances of unmasking potential problems.

Dead-end jobs are often indicated by

- outstanding work being neither recognized nor rewarded,
- a bottleneck to get into management positions, and
- good people leaving the company after obtaining their experience.

If a company is growing and management is expected to double in size over the next five years, there will be opportunities for good workers to move up. If a company is downsizing, or the company's growth is stagnant and management is not close to turning over due to retirement, this is a good indication that no matter how hard you work you are not going to move as far and as fast as you might elsewhere. Research the future outlook and growth for your own employer and any prospective employers.

Companies that impose and enforce unrealistic rules limit the creativity and independence of their workforce. If you feel stifled by your company, there is probably a company out there that will better meet your needs and make you happier in the long run.

If you have a goal to work from a home office, and your current employer does not allow employees to work from home, and you doubt they ever will, you may want to broach the subject with your boss. If you receive a negative response, you may want to start looking around for another employer. Be sure to stay long enough to obtain the experience necessary to make the jump.

Just because a company does not have any employees working from home does not mean that they would not be open to the idea of you working from a home office if you approach it correctly. If you are well entrenched in the company, have a good reputation, would be hard to replace, and you could do just as good of a job from home without any detriment to the company, it may be time to sit down and talk about it with your boss.

Many women who have dreamed of having a home office don't talk to their bosses about it until they become pregnant. I've seen many women ask and be granted home offices while pregnant. Being able to work out of a home office while pregnant is definitely a luxury. If you get tired, you can lay down for half an hour and make it up later in the day. If you are suffering from nausea, it's much nicer to be sitting on a nice clean fluffy bath mat on the floor of your own bathroom, rather than in a dirty public rest room. All of these at-home benefits will make you a happier and more productive employee.

If you are well entrenched in the company, do not wait until you are pregnant to broach the subject of working from a home office. Pregnancy is hard enough. If you can establish your home office routine, get coworkers accustomed to your working from home, and establish that you get just as much done from home prior to becoming pregnant, you'll be better off in the long run. Many people believe that when they cannot see you working, you probably aren't working as hard as you would in an office setting. To overcome these individuals' biases towards home office workers, you'll actually need to work harder than you did in the office and toot your own horn a little. This will win over some of the biased individuals, but probably not all of them. You cannot make everyone happy. Do not dwell on it. Just be sure to win over the decision makers, those who have an impact on your salary and promotions.

Do not be unrealistic about your expectations for a home office. Entry-level positions and new employees often need the daily interaction and supervision from others to achieve the largest learning curves. Obtaining a home office too early in your career can limit the paths available to you in your future. In addition, not all professions have positions that are suitable to being conducted from home. Home offices are discussed in more detail later in this book.

Just as you would when asking to work from a home office, when asking to work part time or flextime, make sure that you have your arguments ready before you walk through the door. Again, it's going to depend on the company's and your boss's attitude.

# Personal Characteristics

Everyone was created equally in the eyes of the law. Not everyone was created equally when it comes to marketable skills. Intelligence, common sense, attitude, ambition, self-esteem, and assertiveness add value to employees. A lack of the correct mix of personality characteristics can significantly decrease the value of an employee. Know your strengths and weaknesses.

## INTELLIGENCE

Depending upon whom you listen to, intelligence can be affected by a number of factors, including genetics, environment, and the luck of the draw. Intelligence is a very important dynamic in moving up the ladder in most professions. However, a lack of a "gift" in a specific field does not rule out that profession as a viable alternative. In many professions, education, experience, and hard work can overcome the lack of a gift. Of course, there are a few fields that require the super-genius gifted types. Generally, these fields are so advanced that a normal person cannot begin to understand them, nor would most have any interest in learning about them.

## COMMON SENSE

Common sense is generally thought of as a trait that people are either born with or not (to varying degrees). I do not know of any class that claims to improve an individual's common sense. However, life experiences can essentially improve common sense. This is especially true in professions with repetitive responsibilities.

Individuals with low common sense in professions requiring high common sense (professions that require individuals to adapt to new situations daily or to deal with unforeseen emergency situations) will not move up within their chosen profession.

## ATTITUDE (OPTIMISM/PESSIMISM)

Where you can go and how much you can achieve is based on your level of optimism. Optimists achieve more than pessimists. They see more opportunities, believe more of those opportunities to be achievable, take more chances, and statistically have a better chance of achieving. Optimists, upon failing, will learn from their failures and later take advantage of other opportunities.

Having a spouse who is an optimist is also important for achieving your goals. Without a spouse's support, it is very tough to take chances and make significant strides.

On the other hand, pessimists are not achievers. They do not recognize opportunities as achievable, and therefore, they never take chances.

## AMBITION/MOTIVATION

Another trait that impacts how achievable one's goals are is ambition (how badly you want to achieve a goal, and what you are willing to do to achieve that goal). When a person is not very ambitious, she will set low goals. When a person is highly ambitious, she will set very high goals. People with low ambition will tend to lower their goals over time. People with high ambition will tend to raise their goals.

Whether you are highly ambitious or not, you will have down days where you just do not feel like doing it again today. On those days, remember what your goal is and why it is important to you. Try not to get down and off track. Salesmen use various motivational techniques to keep the juices flowing. Find ways to motivate yourself to keep going (a day at the spa, time to read a novel, etc.). You cannot be going all the time. Be sure to give yourself some time to recoup and play, or just be lazy.

On the flip side, too much ambition can be a detrimental trait. The source of your ambition or motivation should be evaluated. When it stems from a desire to reach a worthwhile outcome, that's good. When competition is the motivating factor, such as competing with the Smiths or wanting a better position than a friend, then the reasoning behind your goal may be faulty, and you should reevaluate. People motivated by competition (including those who compete against themselves) tend to lose sight of the other important goals in their lives. In addition, they are more likely to push their bodies to the extreme (high stress and late nights). If the body is pushed too hard, it will retaliate, and so will your family.

## SELF-ESTEEM

Professional women invest a significant amount of time obtaining the professional knowledge needed to excel, but the most important factor impacting their futures generally receives very little attention, if any. That most important factor is self-esteem. As pointed out earlier, self-esteem is the single most important factor for a woman's happiness and her earnings potential. Good self-esteem almost guarantees a woman's happiness. Professional women with high self-esteem were more than twice as likely to earn more than $75,000 a year. Professional women with both high self-esteems and high assertive skills were three times as likely to earn more than $75,000 a year.

### What Is Self-Esteem?

To have a good self-esteem is to have an objective unbiased respect for oneself. Women with high self-esteem do not believe they are perfect, nor do they beat themselves down over unimportant or trivial events. They feel good about themselves, accept themselves for who they are, and trust their own judgement.

Women with high self-esteem come in all shapes, sizes, and colors. They accept themselves for who they are inside, rather than what they look like. Their high self-esteem is evident in how they relate to others, in what they believe they are capable of achieving, and in the important decisions that they have made in their lives.

### Identifying and Improving Your Self-Esteem.

There is already a great book on the market that is dedicated to evaluating and improving four areas that are very important to the well-being and growth of all women. That book is *She Who Dares Wins* by Eilleen Gillibrand and Jenny Mosley.[27] The book has four chapters: "Building Self-esteem," "Dealing with Stress," "Developing Assertive Behavior," and "Developing Management Skills."

The self-esteem and assertiveness tests given to the study participants came directly from *She Who Dares Wins*. Rather than reinventing the wheel in my book, I am highly recommending that you read this book and take the time to follow their step-by-step guide about how to improve in these areas.

Their chapter on self-esteem begins by providing self-esteem tests for both your personal and professional lives. The tests provide you with an overall score and category for your self-esteem, as well as identifying the areas where you could use improvement. Once you have identified the areas giving you the most trouble, you are provided with the information necessary to improve your self-esteem. Topics include:

---

27. Eilleen Gillibrand and Jenny Mosley, *She Who Dares Wins* (London: Harper Collins, 1995).

- enhancing your self-image,
- changing negative thought patterns,
- recognizing self-created myths,
- believing in your positive qualities,
- accepting your faults,
- liking and respecting yourself,
- taking care of your own needs (including fulfilling your spiritual self, cognitive self, physical self, creative self, and emotional needs),
- evaluating your real potential, and
- maintaining a balanced view of your life.

Completing the tests and exercises, then implementing the strategies to make changes in your everyday life, will result in a higher self-esteem. However, do not expect overnight results. The exercises take time to complete. Reconditioning your thoughts and changing your natural responses to specific types of events will take time. One's self-image cannot be instantly changed. It's going to take an investment in yourself. In the end, you will be a much better person for it.

### Areas of Low Self-Esteem Identified
### Among All Study Participants

- 57% of the women had trouble giving themselves time for special treats. Women lose their self-identity when they make time for everyone else, but they don't take time to meet their own needs and desires.
- 50% of the women believed that they never or only sometimes used their talents and capabilities. However, this figure was much higher (75%) among the homemakers. One of the homemakers responded that this figure was higher among homemakers because homemakers are willing to

not use their talents and capabilities to their full potential for the benefit of their children. Taking the homemakers out of the calculation still results in a significant 43% of the working women believing that they never or only sometimes use their talents and capabilities.

- 48% often (or always) felt they had to try to impress people with their capabilities.
- 34% of the participants often had trouble relaxing and having fun.
- 34% tried to please other people almost all the time.
- 32% of the participants had trouble trusting most people.
- 30% tried too often to impress people with their appearance.
- 28% of participants had trouble admitting to making mistakes.
- 26% often or always tried to keep problems to themselves. Of course, there are always individuals on the other end of the spectrum who tell their problems to everyone.
- 24% of participants worried too often about what people might think about them.

There was no correlation identified between the profession that a woman entered and her self-esteem. For example, the attorneys who participated in the study had the same average self-esteem score as the average study participant. However, because the study participants came from so many different professions, the sample sizes for the various professions become too small to be relied upon with any degree of certainty.

Of the study participants, only 7% scored in the top tier of the self-esteem categories. One third of those participants were homemakers and two thirds were part-time workers. Not one full-time worker scored in this top tier category. The question then arises, "Why were there no full-time workers in the very highest self-esteem category?" Here are a few of the hypotheses that I have heard:

- Women with lower self-esteem are more likely to fear the unknown. They have a tough time making changes in their lives and therefore are less likely to make the jump to working part time or becoming a homemaker.
- Full-time working women are juggling so many professional and personal responsibilities that they are more likely to lose themselves in the process.
- Women with lower self-esteem are more likely to use work as a crutch for establishing their identity. These same women pay little attention to boosting their personal identities.

I do not necessarily agree with any of these hypotheses, but they do provide fodder for thought and future discussion. Even though the full-time working women were not in the top category, they did overall have fairly good self-esteem.

### Self-Esteem and the Professional Woman

Too many women have low self-esteem. Whether it's an inherent trait or something that develops from environment and experiences, women need to raise their feelings of self-worth in order to empower themselves to win. Lower self-esteem is the number one reason why women fail. We tend to be our own worst enemies, undermining ourselves without knowing it. Positive thinking and challenging our tendencies towards negative thoughts is the beginning of self-empowerment. But as stated earlier, these changes take time and effort.

Most of our mothers, while being great role models for so many facets of our lives, were not given the opportunities to become the professionals that we have the opportunity to become today. While telling us we could be anything we wanted to be, most couldn't provide the road map that would show us what we needed to do to get there (other than telling us to go to college and to work hard). Our largest void has been the missing female role model who could show us how to handle ourselves in the professional world. Did you ever see your mother speak publicly, other than at PTA meetings? Did she ever bring home the sticky situations she encountered at work and explain how she handled them? Most mothers didn't because it was not part of their life experience. So now that we are here, we have to learn these things on our own.

*Upon graduating from college, it is natural to question your abilities and to lose some self-confidence.* You are entering an unknown environment. Over time, your self-confidence will rise. However, maintaining an appearance of self-confidence is important, even when you are not feeling very confident.

*Perception is everything.* People will not believe in you if they don't believe that you believe in yourself first. The key is to fake self-confidence until you have achieved it. That does not mean that you should be boastful or act snooty. It means that your actions and deeds should always show that you are confident in whatever you are doing. It's a matter of the true you shining through without showing the weakness of insecurity.

Whatever you are doing, do it with confidence. For example, if you are asking someone for help, speak confidently with the person you are asking the help from. Body language is a very important indicator of self-esteem. Make eye contact, keep your shoulders back, and stand up straight. Do not fidget and be sure to speak clearly. When asking for help, feel self-assured, because you know when to ask for assistance, and you are not too frightened to ask for it. Also have confidence that you will be able to digest the information and grow from it. Entry-level individuals are expected to learn and grow on the job. Speak with self-confidence no matter what level of person you are speaking with. Everyone had a first job and has gone through first job jitters.

*Do not let others affect your self-confidence.* You are in control of your self-confidence and no one else can bring it down or raise it up. You will not be liked by everyone, and not everyone will think you are doing a good job. That's life. If you have done your best, that's it, so don't second-guess it. There isn't an executive out there who didn't make mistakes along the way. We would all change things if we could go back. But we can't, so keep going.

When there are individuals who do not like you or question your ability or give you a hard time, try to figure out the reason behind their actions. If the reason behind their actions points to something you could improve, and if it fits within your goals, go for it. If not, don't worry about it. You will run into a lot of people who will try to put obstacles in your path (whether intentionally or unintentionally). In a few years, you will probably have bypassed them.

When you first begin on your career path, you may be working for low-level managers who have been in the same position for years. These individuals may be frustrated by ambitious young employees moving up past them or moving to better positions with other companies. These managers are often not helpful and could have traits that hold them back. Learn what you can from these individuals, but do not mimic the traits that have halted their rise. Set your sights higher. Just because they are above you now does not make them better. Early on, you may have to put time in with such individuals. That's part of being at the bottom and working your way up.

Throughout life you will run into these people. Learn what you can, keep your self-confidence up, and move on. In high school, I had a career counselor assigned to me who said some things that would have stopped most individuals from applying to college. When I was accepted at a school, she told me how surprised she was that I was accepted there, and that I would have a tough time academically surviving. I not only survived, but graduated with a 4.0 in my major. I then went on to Villanova Law's Graduate Tax Program where I graduated at the top of my class. The lesson is that I needed that high school career counselor to send my transcripts to the schools to which I applied, but I did not need to accept her advice concerning alternatives to going to college. I had confidence in my future, and I wasn't going to let a nincompoop affect my self-esteem.

At my first job out of college, one of my peers was an over-forty woman that all too often commented on how young people today want too much too quickly, have too many ambitions, and cannot possibly achieve all they plan to. She often cut out newspaper articles that sided with her position. One of the articles that I still remember her showing me stated that new college graduates were too ambitious, too lazy, expected to earn an unrealistic amount by the time they were thirty years old, and needed to be introduced to the real world where they would be taken down a notch. It's a good thing I didn't listen to her. By the time I was thirty, I had surpassed the amount that the article thought was unrealistic. Being young is the time to be ambitious, take chances, and hold onto your self-confidence. If you do not believe in yourself, no one else will.

*Never give your power away.* You'll just be empowering someone else. Most women do not recognize when they are giving their power to other people. If you have been empowered to perform a project, don't be weak. It is acceptable to ask for opinions when needed, listen to answers, and then make the decision for yourself. However, do not give the project or decision to someone else. On the other hand, wanting too much control and not being able to delegate or function as part of a team is also a weakness.

*Reinforce the positives:* I am a good person, being a woman is great, there are no limitations that I cannot overcome, I can do it, I deserve it, and my appearance is just fine.

*Everything you do contributes to how others perceive your self-confidence,* from the way you answer your phone to your voice mail message to how you hold your body. Evaluate how others may be perceiving you with what you'd like them to see.

When you make a mistake, acknowledge that you made the mistake and highlight what you have learned from the experience. It is not a sign of weakness to acknowledge that you made a mistake and take responsibility for it. Learning is part of moving up. Everyone, including the CEO's of the top fifty U.S. companies, make mistakes all the time. It's the people who do not learn from their mistakes that never move up.

*Don't whine and don't gossip.*

## ASSERTIVENESS

Assertive skills are extremely important to professional women. Poor assertive skills lead to

- poor communication,
- improper handling of aggressive behavior,
- improper handling of criticism,
- improper handling of praise and compliments,
- not being able to ask for what you want,
- not being able to say no, and
- not being able to communicate assertively when it is called for.

## What Is Assertiveness?

Assertive behavior is not aggressive and not manipulative. Assertive behavior is actually the opposite of passive behavior. To be assertive is to communicate your point of view in a well thought out and convincing manner with assurance and confidence, and without the appearance of fear.

People with good assertive skills are capable of asking for increases in their salaries (or school grades) when they believe such increases are due. The fear of a confrontation and the fear of rejection do not hinder women with good assertive skills. Other examples of good assertive skills are

- volunteering for projects that you are capable of doing, and that you have time to complete,
- saying no when appropriate,
- ending a conversation when someone has stepped over the line in the way they are speaking to you,
- speaking up at a meeting,
- giving appropriate feedback at the appropriate time, and
- receiving feedback without being defensive.

## Identifying & Improving Your Assertiveness

As noted earlier, the third chapter in the book *She Who Dares Wins* is dedicated to developing assertive behavior.[28] The authors do a great job of providing a step-by-step guide for becoming more assertive. I highly recommend that you read the chapter dedicated to this topic and follow through on their advice.

The authors provide assertiveness tests for your personal and professional lives. The tests provide you with an

28. Eilleen Gillibrand and Jenny Mosley, *She Who Dares Wins* (London: Harper Collins, 1995).

overall score and identify the areas where you need improvement. Once you have identified the areas giving you the most trouble, you are then provided with the information necessary to improve your assertive skills.

Do not expect overnight results. The exercises take time to complete. Reconditioning your thoughts and changing your natural responses to specific types of events will take time. Becoming assertive is similar to public speaking. It's tough to do at first, but as you do it more and more, it becomes much easier. Make the investment in yourself.

### *Areas Where Low Assertive Behavior Was Identified among All Study Participants*

- 78% of the study participants had trouble giving criticism when it was deserved without aggression or apology.
- 78% had trouble dealing with bossy or domineering colleagues.
- 74% had trouble asking for salary increases when they thought they deserved it.
- 73% had trouble saying no when asked to do something at work that was unfair, too difficult, or outside the terms of their contract.
- 61% didn't always take criticism, which was deserved, well (for lateness, forgetting deadlines, etc.).
- 57% had trouble speaking with someone about unfair criticism or their being put down in front of colleagues.
- 54% had trouble giving opinions when they were against what most people thought.
- 51% had trouble putting themselves forward when there was an opportunity for promotion.

# Spousal Support

Meeting your expectations and goals is a long and tough road. However, the road becomes nearly impassible when your spouse neither believes in nor supports your aspirations.

The happiness portion of the study showed that divorced women with children were the least happy group of professional women. The first step to avoid such problems is to marry the right man (if you decide to marry at all). The second step is to invest in the marriage and make it work.

Marrying the right person is a concern for any woman or man about to walk down the aisle. A marriage certificate does not come with a one hundred percent satisfaction guarantee.

There are good days in marriage and bad days in marriage, but most of the days are somewhere in the middle. One woman described most days as "Content exhaustion — like coming home to an old, warm, comfortable pair of slippers on a cold day."

Marriage is work. Anyone entering a marriage believing that every day will be filled with romance and surprises is setting herself up for disappointment. If you have not realized that marriage will not always be easy, then you have not been dating that special person long enough to get married. You will not see the full personality of the person you are dating for at least the first year, with one exception. Truly miserable people generally show their true colors much earlier than others. The problem with women who marry these truly miserable marriage candidates (alcoholics, abusers, liars, philanderers, or lazy individuals) is that these women were generally presented with the signs before they got married, but they chose to ignore them. These women think these men will change when they get married. They won't. These women also think that the marriage will get better after they add children to the mix. It doesn't.

Other marriage candidates to avoid include those that are controlling, uncompromising, not supportive, don't show interest in your goals and aspirations, and those with very low self-esteem.

According to one well-quoted statistic, over 50% of marriages end in divorce. That figure is not accurate and has never been reported by any government agency (including the Census Bureau). The only divorce statistic that is reported by a government agency is that 4.2 of every 1,000 individuals in the U.S. divorce (according to the National Center for Health Statistics). The population contains everyone from newborns to grandmothers.

The 50% divorce rate figure often thrown around is arrived at using the National Center for Health Statistics figures. This agency states that their figures are misused in arriving at that 50% figure, and that they do not support that calculation. In addition, many of the states do not provide any information to the National Center for Health Statistics and are therefore not included in any calculation. Contained within these figures are individuals who have had multiple divorces.

The General Social Survey (GSS) reports that 34 to 36% of Americans have divorced. But other figures show 25% of adults in the U.S. have been divorced. The Census Bureau statistics show that between 9% and 12% of the general population age eighteen and over were divorced (1998). There should be a national study to find out the divorce rate by age, education level, and by those with a history of divorce. Instead, the Census Bureau wastes taxpayer money studying how many toilets are found in American homes. It's important to know the true U.S. divorce rate. However, at this time, it is still unknown.

Among study participants between the ages of twenty-eight and thirty-five, the divorce rate was 3%. When the participants were asked what they would change if they had it to do all over again, only 5% said their spouse. Therefore, of the married study participants, very few believed they made the wrong decision about who they married. Of course, some may argue that these individuals had not been married long enough by their age to know whether they would eventually get divorced.

The problem with the misleading high divorce statistics is that it attempts to normalize divorce. Divorce is a sad predicament when it does occur and a necessary evil at times, but is it really required so often that it should be considered "normal"? Individuals who view divorce as normal are going to be much more likely to get divorced themselves. Marriage is work. It requires good communication, compromise, growth, good listening skills, and fair-mindedness. When problems arise, more than a slight attempt should be made to work things out. Divorce should not be jumped into.

The best advice anyone can give you is not to jump into marriage in the first place. Give it time. After college, your goals and aspirations may change. You will not receive the necessary mental spousal support to meet your goals unless you stay married. In order to stay married, you need to choose the right spouse, and you also need to invest yourself in making the marriage work.

# Recognize Shortcomings & Improve Upon Them

Even highly ambitious individuals need to recognize their limitations and shortcomings in order to reach their goals. After recognizing your shortcomings, determine whether you can improve upon them yourself. You may be able to improve in one area just by concentrating on it. For example, individuals that use slang are often limited in their upward mobility because of their language skills. If you say the word "like" in every other sentence, you could try limiting your use of the word "like." If you tend to interrupt others while they are speaking, you can try to listen more intently and not speak until others have completed their thoughts.

If your shortcomings are of a more technical nature, you should look into improving them through reading journals or books or by attending a class (public speaking, writing skills, etc.). Where you can, improve your technical knowledge, communication skills, public speaking, and management tools.

# CHAPTER 6

# Discrimination

## *Overview*

Everyday we are bombarded with news reports that provide real-life examples of workplace discrimination against women. We all know that discrimination exists. The question is, how prevalent is discrimination against today's professional women?

It is very important that young professional women hold a realistic view of their chances of encountering discrimination. Women who unrealistically believe that discrimination is lurking behind every corner will create their own obstacles to achievement. Women holding such views are more likely to blame their failures on discrimination and believe their failures are someone else's fault. Believing that their future is not under their control, they never learn from their failures. These women are often programmed to fail.

Women who unrealistically believe that discrimination has been completely wiped out will be unprepared if they encounter discrimination. These women will have a tough time recognizing discrimination and responding to it in the moment, and they will be more likely to ignore discrimination when it occurs. Therefore, it is extremely important that today's professional women possess an accurate picture of the discrimination that they can reasonably expect to encounter.

The study of professional women revealed that the majority of well-educated women neither believe that they have been discriminated against, nor do they expect to encounter discrimination in their future. Ninety-four percent of the women in the study stated that discrimination or a glass ceiling has not held them back from achieving all they could have by this point in their lives. Keep in mind that the study is not representative of minorities. There is no question that women from minorities face an increased number of obstacles due to their race.

In addition, many of the mothers who participated in the study stated that they have made choices as mothers to limit their careers for the benefit of their families. They believe that if they would have earned more as men, or would have gone farther up the ladder as men, it would have only been due to their decision to limit their professional lives for their families, not due to discrimination.

The two statistics often used to support the position that discrimination against women is high are:

1. Women earn 75¢ for every dollar earned by men, and
2. women only hold 10% of the senior management positions at Fortune 500 Companies.

On their face, these statistics seem pretty damning; however, a more in-depth review shows that they are the result of many factors, the least of which is actual discrimination. These statistics are very misleading because they do not take into consideration many factors that are not due to discrimination.

However, just because discrimination against professional women is lower than we have been led to believe does not negate the fact that it does exist. Women need to know what constitutes discrimination and be prepared to handle discrimination in the moment. It is very important to learn from the study participants' examples of discrimination. Of the women who encountered discrimination, those who faced it head on and did something about it generally believe that they are not making any less today and do not believe they would be any further along in their careers had they been men. However, the women who encountered discrimination and simply accepted it generally believe they are making less today and are not as far along in their careers due to the discrimination.

High self-esteem and good assertive skills can often circumvent the effects of discrimination. We can be anything we want. We just cannot be everything we want. We control our destinies through the choices we make and the actions we take.

## We've Come a Long Way

Just in the past one hundred years the reduction in discrimination has been astounding. To keep things in perspective about how far we have come, here is an excerpt from the July 1943 issue of *Transportation*:

> There's no longer any question whether transit companies should hire women for jobs formerly held by men. The

draft and manpower shortage have settled that point. The important things now are to select the most efficient women available and to use them to the best advantage. Here are eleven tips on the subject from Western Properties.

1) Pick young married women. They usually have more of a sense of responsibility than their unmarried sisters, are less likely to be flirtatious, still have the pep and interest to work hard and to deal with the public efficiently, and they need the work or they would not be doing it.

2) When you have to use older women, try to get ones who have worked outside the home at some time in their lives. Older women who have never contacted the public have a hard time adapting themselves and are inclined to be cantankerous and fussy. It's always well to impress upon older women the importance of friendliness and courtesy.

3) General experience indicates that "husky" girls — those who are just a little on the heavy side — are more even tempered and efficient than their underweight sisters.

4) Retain a physician to give each woman you hire a special physical examination — one covering female conditions. This step not only protects the property against the possibilities of lawsuit, but reveals whether the employee-to-be has any female weaknesses which would make her mentally or physically unfit for the job.

5) Stress at the outset the importance of time — the fact that a minute or two lost here and there makes serious inroads on schedules. Until this point is gotten across, service is likely to be slowed up.

6) Give the female employee a definite day-long schedule of duties so they'll keep busy without bothering the management for instructions every few minutes. Numerous properties say women make excellent workers when they have their jobs cut out for them, but they lack initiative in finding work themselves.

7) Whenever possible, let the inside employee change from one job to another at some time during the day. Women are inclined to be less nervous and happier with change.

8) Give every girl an adequate number of rest periods during the day. You have to make some allowances for feminine psychology. A girl has more confidence and is more efficient if she can keep her hair tidied, apply fresh lipstick, and wash her hands several times a day.

9) Be tactful when issuing instructions or in making criticisms. Women are often sensitive. They can't shrug off hard words the way men do. Never ridicule a woman — it breaks her spirit and cuts off her efficiency.

10) Be reasonably considerate about using strong language around women. Even though a girl's husband or father may swear vociferously, she'll grow to dislike a place of business where she hears too much of it.

11) Get enough size variety in operator's uniforms so each girl can have a proper fit. This point can't be stressed too much in keeping women happy.

# The Statement That the Average Woman Earns 75¢ for Every Dollar Earned by a Man Is Very Misleading

That figure was calculated by dividing women's median annual earnings by men's median annual earnings for year-round full-time workers (those working over thirty-five hours a week). This figure is useless since it compares apples to oranges. There are many factors other than discrimination that account for the discrepancy. These factors need to be removed from the calculation before a true wage gap due to discrimination can be reported.

Throughout this chapter, part-time work is sometimes identified as working less than thirty-five hours a week, while at other times it is identified as working less than forty hours a week. The difference in reporting is due to the Census Bureau's statistics reporting part-time work as less than thirty-five hours a week, while the study of young professional women considered part-time work as less than forty hours a week.

## HOURS WORKED

The calculation of the 75¢ figure comes from the comparison of the median incomes of women who work more than thirty-five hours a week with the median incomes of men who work more than thirty-five hours a week. The number of hours actually worked is not taken into consideration. Therefore, an individual who works sixty-five hours a week and an individual who works thirty-five and a half hours a week can have their earnings compared with each other.

It's an undisputed fact that the average woman works fewer hours than the average man.[29] The main reason for women working fewer hours than men is children. Eighty percent of women bear children. Of those women with children, many choose to work fewer hours for the benefit of their families.

It's also an undisputed fact that, on average, the more hours someone works, the more income they will receive. Of the study participants who worked between forty and

---

29. U.S. Department of Labor, Bureau of Statistics, "Highlights of Women's Earnings in 1998," report 928 (April 1999). According to the figures released by the U.S. Department of Labor in "Highlights of Women's Earnings in 1998," 70% of the hours worked by people working part time (less than thirty-five hours per week) were worked by women. Forty-three percent of the hours worked by people working full time (more than thirty-four hours per week) were worked by women. The U.S. Department of Labor stated this another way when they wrote: "Women who worked part-time — that is, less than 35 hours per week — represented 25.8% of all female wage and salary workers in 1998. In contrast, 10.7% of men in wage and salary jobs worked part-time." Either way, the average woman works fewer hours than the average man.

fifty hours per week, 16% earned more than $75,000 a year. Of the participants who worked more than fifty hours per week, 47% earned more than $75,000 a year.

Therefore, one of the reasons that the 75¢ figure is inaccurate is that a woman who earns the same hourly rate as a man, but works fewer hours than that man, incorrectly appears to be the victim of wage discrepancy. For example, comparing a woman who works forty hours and earns $40,000 with a man who works fifty hours and earns $50,000 would show that the woman was earning 80¢ for every dollar made by that man. However, the woman and man are actually earning the same hourly rate.

The Census Bureau actually provides comparisons of women's to men's incomes based upon the hours that they worked. However, these more accurate figures still do not provide the complete picture because they do not take into consideration the other non-discriminating factors that impact the wage gap. These other factors are addressed later.

One statistic that was never reported by the mainstream media was, **"Among part-time hourly workers, women earned more per hour than men."** This statement appeared in the Women's Bureau, U.S. Department of Labor's "The Wage Gap Between Women and Men," 1995. The trend of women making more per hour for part-time work continues today. According to the U.S. Department of Labor's "Highlights of Women's Earnings in 1998," women who worked part time (less than thirty-five hours per week) earned 111% of what men earned. The Bureau then further broke down the part-time workers into groups working in five-hour increments. Only women who worked less than five hours a week earned less than their male counterparts working the same hours.

## Women's Earnings as a Percentage of Men's

| Hours Worked | Percentage |
|---|---|
| 34 hours or less | 111.3% |
| 4 hours or less | 73.4% |
| 5 to 9 hours | 106.2% |
| 10 to 14 hours | 106.6% |
| 15 to 19 hours | 105.1% |
| 20 to 24 hours | 112.3% |
| 25 to 29 hours | 113.5% |
| 30 to 34 hours | 107.4% |

Despite the fact that women earn more per hour for part-time work, there has not been an outcry from men that they are being discriminated against.

When looking at the same kind of hour-for-hour comparison for full-time workers, the wage gap never dropped to the 75¢ figure. For example, when comparing the earnings of women who worked between 35 and 39 hours a week with men who worked similar hours, the women earned 97.7% of what men earned on the average. When comparing women and men who worked 45 to 48 hours a week, women earned 87.1% of what the men made. Comparing a woman's earnings with a man's earnings without looking at the hours they worked is extremely misleading, since women, on the average, tend to work fewer hours than men do.

## AGE

The calculation of the 75¢ figure comes from the comparison of the median incomes of women who work more than thirty-five hours a week with the median incomes of men who work more than thirty-five hours a week. The age of the person performing the work was not taken into consideration.

A woman's age significantly impacts how much she makes in comparison to a man. Older women have less education and less experience than older men. It was not until 1978 that 50% of women were in the labor force. Today's CEO's received their education in the 1960s and 1970s when women accounted for only 4% of graduate degrees in law and business.

In addition, discrimination against women was much higher in the 1960s and 1970s. Therefore, older women in the workforce are going to make less than men their age because they have less education and less experience, and were more likely to have faced previous discrimination. This does not mean that these women, who are making less today because of these past factors, are still being discriminated against today.

The Women's Bureau at the U.S. Department of Labor released a report, "The Wage Gap between Women and Men, 1995." The report found that "the wage gap generally grows with age. In 1995, it was smallest among workers ages twenty to twenty-four. Women in that age category earned 92% of what men earn. Women who are between fifty-five and fifty-nine years old earn 65% of what men earn."

"Young women and men (those under twenty-five) had fairly similar earnings (young women's earnings were about 91% of men's); however, women's earnings were much lower than men's in older age groups."[30] Therefore, comparing a woman's earnings with a man's earnings without taking into consideration the age of the participants is extremely misleading.

---

30. U.S. Department of Labor, Bureau of Statistics, "Highlights of Women's Earnings in 1998," Report 928 (April 1999).

## PAST WORK EXPERIENCE

Past work experience was not taken into consideration when calculating the 75¢ figure.

As stated earlier, the average working woman works fewer hours than the average man. In addition, many mothers stop working completely for a while (as homemakers) while their children are young. These women who work part time or become homemakers do not have the same past work experience as other women and men who continued to work full time. In addition, part-time work is often comprised of more routine jobs, and companies are less likely to invest in costly training for part-time employees.

Economist Jane Waldfogel from Columbia University in New York City has found that both men and women having a nontraditional employment history (including part-time work experience) is associated with lower current wages and benefits.[31] Therefore, since more women have nontraditional employment histories than men, women are more likely to make less on the average.

Eighty percent of all women bear children at sometime in their lives, and a quarter of all women work part time. In 1994, June O'Neill of the City University of New York (the former Director of the Congressional Budget Office) reported that twenty-seven- to thirty-three-year-old women who have never had a child earn 98% of the amounts their male counterparts earn.[32] Jane Waldfogel found that among women who work while pregnant, those who quickly return to their pre-birth employer experience faster wage growth than those who do not (nearly as fast as

31. Marianne Ferber and Jane Waldfogel, "The Long-Term Consequences of Non-Standard Work," *Monthly Labor Review*, 121(5), (1998): 3–12. Marianne Ferber and Jane Waldfogel (in press) "The Effects of Part-Time and Self-Employment on Wages and Benefits: Differences by Race/Ethnicity and Gender," in Francois Carre, Marianne Ferber, Lonnie Golden, and Steve Herzenberg (eds.), *The Rise of Nonstandard Work Arrangements: Dimensions, Causes, Consequences, and Institutional Responses* (Ithaca: Industrial Relations Research Association and Cornell University Press).

32. June O'Neill, "The Shrinking Pay Gap," *Wall Street Journal*, (October 7, 1994): A10.

the women who remain childless). However, women who leave the workforce lose seniority and experience to male workers who have uninterrupted careers.[33]

Since the average working woman has less experience than the average man, such experience should also be taken into consideration when calculating the wage gap due to discrimination. Otherwise, a woman's past choice to become a homemaker or to work part time will make it look like women are earning less due to discrimination, when it is actually due to choices that these women made.

Several articles argue that many women have to stay at home or work part time because of pressures from society and their husbands. Women who rely on such theories need to get a backbone. It's a woman's choice to pick the person she marries, it's a woman's choice to have children and when to have children, and it's a woman's choice not to work. If a woman decides not to work for family responsibilities, that's wonderful. But in today's society, no one can argue that women are forced to give up working and stay at home because of discrimination. The homemakers that I have studied are proud to stand up and say they chose to be at home, and that they made such decisions in order to provide the best start for their children. *None* of the homemakers who participated in the study became homemakers because of society's pressures and discrimination.

Other articles argue that because most men and most women view the husband's career as the primary career and the wife's career as a secondary career that this is society's internal discrimination. They further conclude that women are put at a disadvantage because families will not move to another state for a wife's career, thereby limiting

---

33. Jane Waldfogel, "The Family Gap for Young Women in the United States and Britain: Can Maternity Leave Make a Difference?" *Journal of Labor Economics* 16(3) (1998): 505–545. Jane Waldfogel, "Working Mothers Then and Now: A Cross-Cohort Analysis of the Effects of Maternity Leave on Women's Pay," in Francine Blau and Ronald Ehrenberg (eds) *Gender and Family in the Workplace* (New York: Russell Sage, 1997).

her potential income. This is not discrimination. Again, it's due to choices. Women often choose to put their families in front of their careers. They also choose their husbands. Choosing to be a wimp and to give into the will of others is also a choice and is not discrimination.

## EDUCATION

Education was not taken into consideration when calculating the 75¢ figure.

"The wage gap is smallest between women and men with masters and doctoral degrees."[34] Therefore, the more education, the lower the wage gap becomes. In the past, fewer women went to college and graduate school than men. Today, more women are attending college than men. In the United States, women earn 56% of the bachelor's degrees and 57% of the master's degrees. However, there are still more women than men in the workforce with lower education levels. Therefore, to compare apples to apples, the 75¢ figure needs to be recalculated comparing women and men with the same education level.

The lower wage gap between men and women who are more highly educated could be partially due to the fact that educated women tend to postpone children for several years. They remain in the workforce for a longer time, providing more uninterrupted time to move up the professional ladder.

## PROFESSION CHOSEN

The professions that the women and men chose were not considered when calculating the 75¢ figure. Women more often than men choose to enter professions that pay less. In the past,

---

34. The Women's Bureau at the U.S. Department of Labor, *The Wage Gap Between Women and Men* (Washington D.C., 1995), Section IV.

women have received more degrees in public administration and communications than men. Of course, the fields women are entering are becoming more diverse. However, more women than men are still choosing to enter nursing and teaching knowing that these professions may not pay the high dollars that some other professions do. Women are not being forced into these professions. These women are choosing these professions because it is what they want to do.

When the U.S. Department of Labor compared the incomes of men and women in the same professions, there were several professions where the wage gap was very small. Had the Department of Labor taken into account the other factors (such as hours worked) that are not related to discrimination, these gaps would have been even smaller. The Department of Labor reported that "as registered nurses, women earn 96.9% of what men earn."[35] In addition, the Department of Labor reports that in the **industries of environmental and architecture, on average, women ages thirty-five to forty-four make more than men.** Findings from the study titled *Free Markets, Free Choices II: Smashing the Wage Gap and Glass Ceiling Myths* include that in architecture and environmental design, young women earn 95% of young men's earnings; in engineering they earn 99%, in chemistry 97%, and in computer and information sciences they earn 94%.[36]

In addition, a small population of the women in the Villanova study said they would have made different decisions in their professional lives had they been born men, since as men they would have felt more responsible for bringing in the family income. Only 3% of the participants believe this to be true for themselves. They wrote:

---

35. The Women's Bureau at the U.S. Department of Labor, *The Wage Gap Between Women and Men* (Washington D.C., 1995), Section VI.

36. Naomi Lopez, *Free Markets, Free Choices II: Smashing the Wage Gap and Glass Ceiling Myths* (San Francisco: Pacific Research Institute).

If I were a man "I feel that my career drive would have been stronger and pushed me."

*

"I would feel increased pressure to provide for my family and would not settle for income in the 30's from my full time job. As it stands, my spouse earns 4 times my income and I do not have pressure to get a different job."

*

"If I were a man, I would have been much more career focused knowing that my future would need me to provide for a family."

An individual's profession should be considered when calculating any wage differential between men and women. Today's woman can choose to enter any profession she wants. She is not limited. She has choices.

## OTHER CHOICES THAT WOMEN MAKE TO OBTAIN OR MAINTAIN FAMILY-FRIENDLY POSITIONS

Many women make conscious decisions (other than just limiting the hours they work) to limit their income or the positions that they obtain in order to obtain or maintain family-friendly positions. The decisions that these women make were not taken into consideration when calculating the 75¢ figure.

Like many of the study participants, I also made decisions for the benefit of my family that will limit my potential income and the positions I will hold in the future. These choices I made freely and are not related at all to discrimination.

I have what I consider the perfect family position. I work for a Fortune 500 Company in the Tax Department. I have a home office in New Jersey. My boss and the rest of the corporate office are in Portland, Oregon. I have a two-year-old daughter and a son due in August. My mother (who lives a mile away) watches my daughter at my house during the day while I work in my home office upstairs. Anytime I want to visit or take a break, I can. On nice days, we go to the park during lunch. On snowy days, we have been known to build snowmen.

Several months ago I had a discussion with the CFO from my company. He explained that the Vice President of the Tax Department would be retiring in a few years, and if I wanted to be considered for this position, I would need to work out of the corporate office. This would mean giving up my home office and having someone other than my mother watch my daughter. I have the background of someone who would be considered for the position: CPA, IRS experience, Master's of Taxation, and Big 5 experience. However, I would not be able to take on more management responsibility and show I was suitable for the position without moving. It made sense that I would only be considered for the position if I gave up my home office. The CFO was not guaranteeing the position, but he was pointing out the path I would need to take if becoming the Vice President of the Tax Department was an aspiration of mine.

It was my decision to make. My present situation was too perfect, and my career aspirations were no longer as important as providing the best family life. Therefore, I made the decision (and my husband concurred) to limit where I could go and to limit what I would make for the quality of my family's life.

Economist Jane Waldfogel from Columbia University in New York City has found that working women with children tend to earn less than working women without children, even among women with the same education and work experience. The average mother's discount appears to be about 10%.[37]

---

37. Jane Waldfogel, "The Effect of Children on Women's Wages," *American Sociological Review* 62, (1997): 209–217.   Jane Waldfogel, "Understanding the 'Family Gap' in Pay for Women with Children," *Journal of Economic Perspectives* 12(1), (1998): 137–156.

A significant portion of the mother's discount is due to choices that mothers make and not discrimination against mothers.

However, having children does not have to limit a woman's income. The following figures appeared in *Fortune* magazine's story "Tales of the Trailblazers."[38] It found that more female Harvard Business School graduates are having children without giving up income. It all depends upon the choices that women make.

| **Average Total Compensation for Harvard Mothers Working Full Time** | | |
|---|---|---|
| | **Class of 1973** | **Class of 1983** |
| Percentage Who Are Mothers | 53% | 70% |
| With Children | $116,714 | $255,725 |
| Without Children | $299,900 | $190,639 |

Sixty-nine percent of the Villanova University alumni study participants had their professional goals change after they had children. Comparing a woman's earnings with a man's earnings without taking into consideration the other choices that mothers make to limit their income is also extremely misleading.

Many recent studies have shown that working women take on more of the household management chores than their male counterparts. Many of the women studied do the extra work around the house because they are assured it will get done to their standards. Other women feel forced into performing the extra work because their husbands would never do the chores on a regular basis. This is not discrimination. Women who take on more chores than

38. Betsy Morris and Ann Harrington, "Tales of the Trailblazers," sub-heading "Having Kids is Okay," *Fortune* 138(7) (October 12, 1998): 106+.

their husbands make a decision to do so. If a woman wants
to give up some of her regular chores, she has many options
including (but not limited to) discussing her concerns with
her husband, going on strike, or hiring a cleaning service.
Once children enter the mix, women often take on a larger
portion of the other household management responsibilities (such as making doctor appointments, verifying that
homework is completed, and planning birthday parties).
Again, this is a choice.

## SELF-EMPLOYED

The Census Bureau's figures do not include the self-
employed. Businesses owned by women are being started at
a faster rate than businesses owned by any other population
segment (from the latest Census Bureau statistics); they
tend to be very profitable, and some surveys estimate that
by the year 2000 half of American businesses will be owned
by women.

Here are some facts based on research and analysis by
the National Foundation for Women Business Owners:

- As of 1999, there were 9.1 million women-
  owned businesses in the U.S., employing over
  27.5 million people and generating over $3.6
  trillion in sales. Firms owned by women now
  account for 38% of all firms in the U.S.
- Between 1987 and 1999, the number of
  women-owned firms increased by 103%
  nationwide, employment increased by 320%,
  and sales grew by 436%.
- 26% of the women-owned businesses in the
  U.S. have their own Web site, compared with
  16% of male-owned businesses (1997 survey).
- Women-owned businesses grew over one and a

half times faster than businesses overall from
1987 to 1999.

- According to their study, the key reason that
  many women are leaving corporate work is
  that they are looking for flexibility. For many,
  that means balancing work and family
  responsibilities.
- When female business owners were surveyed
  in 1994, they said their number one problem
  was that they were not taken seriously. A
  recent survey found that the top issue now is
  managing and maintaining business growth,
  just like any other business. Big corporations
  can no longer ignore female-owned businesses.
  There are too many of them, they have
  become too big, and they are too profitable
  to ignore.

In addition, many of these female entrepreneurs are
moms (mompreneurs).

## MEDIAN VERSUS MEAN

The 75¢ for every dollar was calculated by dividing
women's median annual earnings by men's median annual
earnings for year-round full-time workers. The reason for
using median over mean is that the Census Bureau generally reports figures in median rather than mean. The difference between median and mean could be significant to
these calculations.

The median is calculated by placing the incomes in
order from lowest to highest and then identifying the
income that is halfway from the bottom and top of the list.
The mean is calculated by taking the total incomes of the
women and dividing it by the number of women in the
sample.

The inherent problem with using the median is that it does not provide a true average, and therefore no one can honestly rely on these figures to support the statement that the average full-time working woman earns 75% of what a man makes. Assume the census reviews five men. They earn $15,000, $20,000, $50,000, $50,000 and $65,000. The median income would be $50,000 and the mean income would be $40,000. If five women were then polled and found to earn $15,000, $30,000, $40,000, $50,000, and $65,000, the median salary would be $40,000 and the mean would be $40,000. Using these figures, women would earn 80% of what men earn using median incomes, and women would earn 100% of what men earn utilizing the mean calculation.

Since, the Census Bureau does not report the mean incomes necessary to perform the calculation, we have no way to determine whether the wage gap would go up or down using means. Future wage gap calculations need to compare apples to apples (take out the factors that account for wage differences that are not due to discrimination) and should be calculated with mean incomes.

## THE TRUE WAGE GAP THAT IS DUE TO DISCRIMINATION

The calculation of 75¢ on the dollar does not take into account hours worked, age, past work experience, education, profession chosen, and the other choices women make to obtain and maintain family-friendly positions. None of these factors is due to current discrimination, and therefore they need to be accounted for in the calculation. Many of these factors are due to the choices that women make. In addition, the figure is misleading because it relies on median earnings rather than the mean earnings.

The question then arises, taking these factors into consideration: What is wage gap due to current discrimination practices? It's a matter of comparing men and women with equal training, experience, aspirations, and job choices. The more similar the backgrounds, the closer the earnings. For example, June O'Neill (Wollman Professor of Economics, Baruch College, City University of New York and former Director of the Congressional Budget Office) found that twenty-seven- to thirty-three-year-old women who have never had a child earn 98% of the amounts their male counterparts earn.[39]

A very substantial factor impacting women's wages is children. On the average, women who do not have children earn more money than their childless counterparts. This is supported by data from the study of Villanova alumni women. Of the participants who worked full time (more than forty hours per week), 25% earned more than $75,000 a year. However, of the participants who worked full time and who did not want to have children in their future (and had no children), 40% earned more than $75,000 a year.

Based on her analysis of many data sources, June O'Neill believes that the wage gap estimated for all women, including those with children, is in the range of 0 to 10%. Quantifying the true percentage adjusted for all the relevant differences between men and women is extremely difficult because it is exceedingly tough to measure the decisions and choices that many women make for the benefit of their children and their families. For example, it would take a very detailed study to calculate the impact that my choices to retain family-friendly positions (such as working from a home office over pursuing the position of Vice President of Tax) have had on my income. However, I

---

39. June O'Neill, "The Shrinking Pay Gap," *Wall Street Journal* (October 7, 1994): A10.

am confident that such an in-depth study will be conducted at sometime in the future.

If you are interested in reading more about American women succeeding in the marketplace, read Diana Furchtgott-Roth (of the American Enterprise Institute) and Christine Stolba's (Emory University) book, *Women's Figures: An Illustrated Guide to the Economic Progress of Women in America.*

# The Statement That Women Hold Only 10% of the Senior Management Positions at Fortune 500 Companies Is Also Very Misleading

It takes a lot to rise to the top positions at Fortune 500 Companies. On the average, the individuals holding these positions have MBA's and twenty-five or more years of uninterrupted work experience. If we could theoretically determine the percentage of women who have MBA's and more than twenty-five years of uninterrupted work experience, that would provide the percentage of women we would expect to find holding senior management positions at Fortune 500 Companies, assuming no discrimination held those women back.

Twenty-five years ago, fewer than 7% of MBA graduates were women.[40] Of those MBA candidates, we must assume that at least a few of them worked part time or became homemakers. Therefore, the percentage of women with MBA's and twenty-five years of uninterrupted work experience is less than 7% of the total U.S. population with that background. Therefore, assuming there was no discrimination, one would expect to find less than 7% of

---

40. Tom D. Snyder, National Center for Education Statistics, *Digest of Education Statistics 1997*, NCES 98-015, (US Department of Education: Washington, D.C., 1997), Table 281.

senior management positions at Fortune 500 Companies filled by women; however, the actual percentage holding these positions is 10%. Therefore, the fact that only 10% of those positions are held by women cannot be attributed to current discrimination against women.

Today, women are recognized for the experience and credentials that they possess, without regard to their sex. In April 2000, I was asked to speak at the House Ways and Means Committee's first ever Congressional Summit on Fundamental Tax Reform. Of the fifteen witnesses ranging from Congressmen to business professionals that day, I was the only woman (7% of the experts were therefore female). I am confident that the House Ways and Means Committee was not practicing discrimination even though 93% of their witnesses were male. It just happened that the experience and credentials needed is more often found among males; however, the percentage of women with the necessary credentials and work experience has risen greatly over the past twenty years, and we will see more women represented in all areas in the future.

## What Is Discrimination & What Are Your Rights?

Too many women are unaware of the current laws on the books that are meant to protect them from employment discrimination. This book is a starting point for rectifying that situation. All studies of discrimination should go beyond the preliminary information provided in this book.

When I originally wrote this section, I included many of the Equal Employment Opportunity Commission's (EEOC's) written statements regarding discrimination. However, several of the individuals I asked to review this book found that topic extremely dry. I have since moved that information into Appendix 2; however, this is not an indication that the information is not important. All women should be familiar with the information contained in Appendix 2.

Appendix 2 includes the EEOC's statements regarding

- the principal federal statutes prohibiting employment discrimination,
- the discriminatory practices that are prohibited by these laws (including a discussion of compensation discrimination, sexual harassment, and pregnancy-based discrimination),
- when employers are legally responsible for harassment by a supervisor,
- an employee's responsibilities in taking reasonable steps to avoid harm from harassment by a supervisor,
- which employers must comply with these laws, and
- how to file a charge of discrimination.

It's especially important to be familiar with this information because the laws often limit the time frame for filing discrimination charges. If you are either unfamiliar with what constitutes discrimination or the specific time frame allowed for filing charges, you may inadvertently limit your options for recourse. For example, under several of the laws, a charge must be filed with the EEOC before a private lawsuit may be filed in court. Under some circumstances, a charge must be filed with the EEOC within 180 days from the date of the alleged violation in order to protect the charging party's rights.

## Recognizing Discrimination

Several women have asked me, "How would a woman know she received a lower starting salary or raise?" The answer is easy. It is every woman's responsibility to know how much she is worth. She should be familiar with salary studies by profession. She should also interview every few years (even if she is not planning on leaving her current employer) in order to make sure her salary is in line with what others are willing to pay.

Of course, even if a woman does this, there is a chance that a man hired at the same time for the same position and with the same credentials could be offered more money. But if it's significantly more, rest assured they are overpaying the other individual because you are equipped with the knowledge of what you are worth. With extremely low unemployment and stockholders yelling for profits, it's doubtful that you will be shortchanged if you go in with your eyes open. Turnover of good employees is too costly to companies.

Too many women rely on gossip as their sole source that they have been discriminated against. Gossip can be perceived as truth even when it isn't. Look at the source and the actual evidence. Do not hang your hat on rumors. Bad news and rumors travel more quickly than good news. Seldom do people stand around talking about a person's good characteristics. Therefore, never charge discrimination without actual facts and proof.

The study titled *Free Markets, Free Choices II: Smashing the Wage Gap and Glass Ceiling Myths*[41] states:

> According to the U.S. Equal Employment Opportunity Commission (EEOC), fewer than one in five sexual harassment charges results in a meritorious outcome and fewer than one in twenty is found to have reasonable cause. Of sex-based charges, about one in eight charges result in a meritorious outcome. Only one in 25 is found to have reasonable cause. A formal, legal process, based on

41. Naomi Lopez, *Free Markets, Free Choices II: Smashing the Wage Gap and Glass Ceiling Myths* (San Francisco: Pacific Research Institute).

evidence not conjecture, exists to compensate alleged victims and protect them from retaliation. The process also punishes alleged perpetrators and protects them from false claims. Equating seeming disparities in pay to discrimination, without carefully scrutinizing the facts, undermines the important legal protections and processes that have been carefully established.

# Study Results

The study participants cover the full spectrum of beliefs on discrimination, from women who interpret everything every man on earth does as discrimination to women who are extreme anti-feminists. However, most fall somewhere in the middle.

The participants who answered questions indicating that they were discriminated against were encouraged to provide a written explanation of the discrimination that they encountered. Most did. Many of their written responses are provided below. In some instances I provided comments following the participant's response. It's not important that you agree with my comments. It is important that you think it through for yourself. What we eventually learn from the discrimination debate will ultimately benefit future generations.

There are a number of women in the United States who believe they deserved a promotion, raise, or job and didn't get it because they were discriminated against as women. As stated earlier, there is true discrimination out there; however, of those who believe they were discriminated against, some truly did not deserve the promotion, raise, or other benefit. I ran into such an individual while working at my first job out of college. She was loud, angry, loved to gossip, and had been with the organization for years. She told anyone who would listen that women working there were discriminated against, and that she had been discriminated against by being passed up for promotions in favor of men. After being around her for a short time, I realized she had not been discriminated against. She just did not belong in a management position. The same thing occurs with men. There are men out there who believe they deserved a promotion, but were actually passed over because they did not deserve the promotion.

When reviewing the study results, keep in mind that the participants who believe they were discriminated against may include women who claim discrimination, but did not deserve a promotion, raise, and so on. I do not believe the percentage of women who believe they have been discriminated against when they actually did not deserve the promotion or raise in the first place is very high; however, it is something to keep in mind as you read the responses.

## 96% OF THE WOMEN BELIEVE THEY WERE NEVER DENIED A JOB THEY INTERVIEWED FOR BASED ON THE FACT THAT THEY WERE WOMEN

Three of the women who responded that they were denied a job they interviewed for based on the fact they were women wrote the following explanations:

> "I worked at a company where they felt the territory I would have been given (I was in sales at the time) was a little "rough" for me because I was a woman."
>
> Sales is a field where discrimination is more likely to occur (not necessarily by an employer, but by the customers). There are people who will only make purchases from men. Maybe they feel most comfortable dealing with men. If a customer will not see a woman, it's not her company's fault. When this

happens and a woman is paid on commissions, it can be very hard. Yet, many women are setting trail-blazing sales records selling in male-dominated fields.

Many companies have hired women in the past and have found that the women just cannot get into the doors to see the customers due to the customers' bias; however, companies should not make gender-based decisions for these positions.

The woman who answered this question took control of her career and today believes she would not be any farther along or making any more had she been a man.

*

"I had recently had a baby and an older male dentist did not want to sell his practice to me because he felt I 'had my hands full.'"

*

"After I had been out of law school for about 1 1/2 years, I interviewed for an associates position at a law firm. During my interview with the senior partner, the man asked 'Are you considering making law a career?' Quite obviously the man did not want to hire me because he was afraid that I would have children and quit. This is not the person I wanted to work for, so I thanked him for his time and told him I was no longer interested in the job."

I understand this woman's concern with the interviewer's question. She had just come through four years of undergraduate school and three years of law school. In addition, she had invested time to pass the bar exam. The only reason someone would want to know whether law was going to be her career was someone who wanted to know whether she planned on leaving to have children. This interview may have been an indication that there would be obstacles in her future if she decided to take a position with this firm. She went with her instinct and relied on her self-esteem and assertiveness skills to get her through the situation. She took her career future into her hands. It's every woman's responsibility to control her future. If you don't do it, who will?

## 96% of the Women Believe They Were Never Denied a Promotion Based on the Fact That They Were Women

Here are responses from the four women who responded that they were denied a promotion based on the fact that they were women:

"I interviewed for a job once and another manager told me they had spoken to the hiring manager and the hiring manager told him that I gave the best interview and he really wanted to hire me but thought that because I looked "young" and may not be assertive enough, he felt that he needed to hire a male candidate."

If a hiring manager finds that an interviewee was a great interview, but did not show the self-confidence and assertive skills needed in such a position, it makes sense that he would keep looking for another candidate. However, if a hiring manager automatically attributes low assertive skills to a young women, that would be wrong (assuming he would not have attributed low assertive skills to a young man of the same age). In the participant's example, the manager "felt he needed to hire a male candidate." That manager was clearly wrong.

The interviewee had the option of confronting the hiring manager with her impression of the situation;

however, such a decision would need to be made on a case-by-case basis.·

Looking young is definitely an obstacle. I had the same problem when starting out of college. The best advice is to have high self-esteem and to be assertive. Make eye contact. If you do not possess the self-esteem you'd like to have, fake it. Men who look young do not necessarily have an easier time of it than women who look young. Young is young, whether female or male. If you have impressive credentials, you should be able to overcome that obstacle.

\*

"Went to a more progressive and diverse company."

This was a response from a woman who believed she was denied a promotion and given a smaller raise because she was female. This same woman later answered that she would be no farther along in her career today if she were a man, and she would be earning no more if she were a man. She also answered that she did not believe that discrimination or a glass ceiling held her back from being all she could be by this point in her life. The lesson that can be learned from this woman is to control your destiny. Her self-esteem and assertive skills allowed her to change employers. In the end, she arrived at the same place she would have had she been a man. She just took a different path to get there.

\*

"Compared to men who work 65 hours a week with wives at home taking care of children."

If the promotion was given to a man putting in sixty-five hours a week, he probably deserved the promotion. Deciding not to work sixty-five hours a week because you have children at home is a choice, not discrimination. More men than women have a spouse at home taking care of the children full time; however, the number of men who stay at home with their children is expected to increase in the future.

I would be interested in finding out what percentage of the men in top management positions with the Fortune 500 Companies have wives who stay at home with the children versus the percentage of women in those positions who have husbands at home with the children. I assume there is a big difference. Yet, this is not discrimination. It's a woman's choice. As long as more women stay at home or work fewer hours, there will always be more men at the top. And that's okay.

\*

"Tried for my company's marketing department. There wasn't much to be one."

Many who work in marketing departments would disagree with this statement. I know of many companies where there is a lot to making it into a company's marketing department.

## 90% BELIEVE THEY WERE NEVER GIVEN A SMALLER RAISE BECAUSE OF BEING A WOMAN

Six of the women who believed they were given smaller raises gave explanations as follows:

"Talked with my boss and got nowhere. I started looking for another job after that."

Great example of a woman taking control of her life.

\*

"The two years in which I took two 3 month maternity leaves, my raises were smaller than they would have been had I worked a full 12 months."

According to the EEOC: "If an employee is temporarily unable to perform her job due to pregnancy, the employer must treat her the same as any other temporarily disabled employee.... Employers must hold open a job for a pregnancy related absence the same length of time jobs are held open for employees on sick or disability leave."

The EEOC has stated that when a company has a policy where sick or disability absences are taken into account for everyone when determining raises (regardless of the type of sickness or disability), that policy is not considered discriminatory. However, when only the absences of women who have taken maternity leave are taken into account for determining raises, that is discriminatory. For example, assume a man and a woman are employed by the same company, and the man was in an automobile accident and was absent six weeks, and the woman gave birth to a child and took off six weeks for maternity leave. The company cannot implement a policy that only penalizes women. The policy must treat all sick and disabled employees equally.

*

"A typical situation in the corporate advertising industry where male president of company failed to see the importance of my job, and being a female made matters that much worse."

When people question the importance of your job, it's time to turn on your assertive skills. If someone believes your job does not add much value to the company, it's your responsibility to show them the light. No one will sing the praises of the great job that you are doing. Americans are taught not to boast about accomplishments. However, if we don't do it, how will anyone know how important the job that we do is? When needed, self-promotion can be very important to our livelihood. Of course, too much self-promotion or bad timing can also hurt your career. It's a fine line.

Let others know what you are doing and how important what you do is to the company. But do not overdo it. If you don't believe in your position or your value to the company, you can't sell what's not there.

You also can't sell all the people all the time. It's important to sell the ones who matter (those who control raises, promotions, etc.). As the first employee out of 13,000 to work out of a home office, I had a lot of people to sell. Many held the belief that there was no way that just as much work could be done from home. I couldn't sell everyone, but I did prove it to the ones who mattered.

*

"A male colleague and I received the same performance appraisal, yet he got a 9% raise and I got a 5% raise; all else was constant."

*

"Happens regularly – not viewed as sole supporter of family."

There are managers who give better raises to men who are the sole supporters of families. However, it does not happen often anymore. Businesses that want to make money will pay what they have to, to keep good employees. At the same time, companies are in business to make a profit. They are going to try to pay employees the least they reasonably can. For example, assume a company has thirty accountants on staff and they are all paid $25,000 a year. The company then hires ten new accountants. If the new accountants will not come on board for less than $35,000, does that mean that the company should automatically give raises to the thirty other accountants? Absolutely not. If the company assumes those thirty have not kept up with salary surveys and have no idea what accountants can earn, there is little chance those employees will leave.

In this economy, where good employees are in high demand, companies cannot discriminate in favor of men who are viewed as sole supporters of their families. There would be nothing stopping a good female employee from getting another job for better pay. Stockholders do not care what the gender of the employees are. They care that employees add to the company's bottom line.

Be up front and honest. After you have done your homework, tell an employer when they are not paying you a competitive salary, and that you can make more elsewhere.

*

"Due to my pregnancy – I let it go."

## 93% *Believe They Were Never Given a Smaller Starting Salary Because They Were Women*

Four of the women who believed they were given a smaller starting salary because they were women gave explanations as follows:

"I find this ALWAYS happens!!! I did not deal with it – just accepted it."

She should have taken control of the situation. If you are offered a smaller starting salary because you are a woman, keep looking for another job. If you need to take the lower paying job until you find a better paying job, do it.

*

"I especially think that being married and having a husband who works gives employers the idea that you don't need to be paid as much as you're worth because you don't 'need' it, so to speak."

*

"When searching for my first job out of college, all employment agencies had administrative jobs that they did not even offer to men. All the salaries were low. I was frustrated and had to accept it to get a job."

*

"At three companies, I know men were initially offered higher salaries, even though I had a stronger background/experience."

## 91% BELIEVE DISCRIMINATION HAS NOT LIMITED HOW FAR THEY HAVE COME IN THEIR CAREERS

This figure breaks down as follows:

- 73% believed they would not be any farther in their careers today if they had been men.
- 16% believed that if they *were* further along in their careers today, it would only be due to the choices they had made as mothers.
- 2% believed that if they had been farther along in their careers today as men, it would have only been because as men they would have taken more interest in making decisions that would have brought about larger incomes, since they believe men have the burden of being the main family supporters.
- 9% believed that discrimination against them as women had limited how far they had come in their careers.

The women who believed that if they were farther along in their careers today, it would only be due to the choices they had made in their lives as mothers came from a mix of full-time workers, part-time workers, and homemakers. Here are a few representative statements from these women:

"We have a daughter, and as I work one day at home, I have decided not to be as aggressive."

*

"I feel as though I am the only one holding myself back by putting my family first and career somewhat 'on hold' while my kids are young."

*

"If I was a man, I would most likely still be working outside the home."

*

"I have two young children and I feel that being a mother has taken precedence over my career. I would be able to devote more time and energy to my job if I were a man and would probably be making more money if my job were more of a focus for my life. I have made the choice to put my children over my career."

*

"As a woman, the choice of having a family has a direct impact on one's career regardless of whether or not one chooses to take time off from your career."

*

"Yes, because if I was a man I would probably be more dedicated at work, since my primary role is as a mother. I am the one to stay at home with sick kids, leave right at 5:00, etc."

*

"I have 3 children and it is a choice that I made, but if I didn't stop my career 3 times I would be further along."

*

"But only because as a woman, I feel my most important life's work is to be a full-time mom. To do this, I have voluntarily put my career on hold. I do not believe that most men have to or choose to make this decision."

*

"Only because of my infertility related problems — but I was happy to leave my job so I could pursue my dream of being a mother!"

This woman left a full-time stressful job for a less stressful job working eight hours a week, in order to overcome infertility problems. She eventually became pregnant.

*

A woman who now works part-time wrote: "Because when my husband and I started having children I stayed at home. While I do not regret the choice we made, if I were a man I would most likely still be in the workforce full time."

*

"Because women belong home with the kids; i.e.: I gave up my career to raise my children."

The women who believed that discrimination against them as women had limited where they were in their careers today made statements such as the following:

"I still think men are paid more and have more opportunity and certain low level jobs men are not even considered for."

*

"Men that I started with 10 years ago were promoted before me and are much further along in their careers than I am, even though I believe we are equally qualified."

During a good economy, there are very few reasons to stay with such a company. This is a situation where a woman needs to take control. Self-esteem and assertiveness are very important in these situations.

*

"That's just the way it is. Women work harder but men are considered first."

\*

"Men seem to receive more respect in the workplace. Employers seem to take men more seriously than women."

When I first entered the workforce from college, I also thought that men received more respect in the workplace. However, as my self-confidence and my assertive skills grew, I found that women received just as much respect and are taken just as seriously as men when they do a good job, know they did a good job, and are assertive. Even when I run into men who hold antiquated ideas, a good job and experience generally overcomes that impression very quickly.

\*

"Dentistry is a male dominated field."

\*

"Because you are a woman and may leave to start a family some people (men mostly) will take that into consideration when considering raises and promotions."

## 76% BELIEVE THAT DISCRIMINATION HAS NOT IMPACTED WHAT THEY EARN. OF THE PARTICIPANTS WHO BELIEVE THEIR INCOME HAS BEEN LIMITED BY DISCRIMINATION, MANY RELY SOLELY ON THE INACCURATE 75¢ STATISTIC

It broke down as follows:

- 58% believed they would not be making any more if they were men.
- 15% believed that if they were making more today as men, it would only be due to the choices they had made as mothers.
- 3% believed that if they were making more today as men, it would only be due to the fact

that as men they would have taken more interest in making decisions that would have
brought about larger incomes, since they
believe men have the burden of being the main
family supporters.

- 24% believed that discrimination against them
  as women had limited the amount that they
  were earning.

The women who believed that discrimination against them
as women had limited what they earned today made statements such as the following:

> "Rumor that when a male RN was hired at the hospital, his
> starting salary was higher."
>
> Be very careful of rumors. It is very important to
> know how much you are worth without relying on
> gossip. This study participant had no other exam-
> ples of discrimination, other than the belief that
> discrimination had limited what she was earning
> today.
>
> *
>
> "Because I have heard incidents of this happening through
> other people."
>
> Again rumors.
>
> *
>
> "I truly believe men are compensated at a higher rate than
> women, especially in the investment field."
>
> *
>
> "Good old boys network. Women, especially married women,
> don't need the compensation that a man does."
>
> *
>
> "I believe that there is still a tendency for employers to pro-
> mote men because men have traditionally been the 'bread win-
> ners' that have to support families."

\*

"Proven fact."

\*

"Every salary survey shows men earn more than women. Again, I don't know from company salaries because I don't know what others earn."

\*

"Because men who I trained in the Purchasing Department were making more than I was (they volunteered their salary info.) and I had supposedly been 'promoted' to contracts and was making less than the 'Buyers.'"

\*

"In a male dominated profession such as law, I believe that the men I have worked for who decide on salaries, etc. pay their male employees more than the women."

\*

"Though it's getting better, men generally do make more money than women in the same jobs. Odds are that if I were a man, I would have somewhere in my career been making more."

\*

"I think my aggressive behavior/style in promoting myself would have been more readily received if I was a man."

\*

"Men usually make more money."

This study participant had no other examples of discrimination, other than the belief that discrimination had limited what she was earning today.

Many study participants jumped to the conclusion that discrimination against them as women has limited the amount that they would be earning, solely based on statistics that say "women make less than men," and not based on actual knowledge. These participants were unaware that these wage discrepancy statistics do not adjust for factors unrelated to discrimination (such as hours worked and education level).

Women who have the technical knowledge and credentials required in their field, high self-esteem, good assertive skills, and who know how much they are worth can feel comfortable in the fact that they are not being paid less than their male peers.

## 94% BELIEVE THAT DISCRIMINATION OR A GLASS CEILING HAS NOT HELD THEM BACK FROM ACHIEVING ALL THEY COULD HAVE BY THIS POINT IN THEIR LIVES

The women who believed that discrimination or a glass ceiling had prevented them from achieving all they could have made statements such as the following:

"This has not affected me significantly, but I honestly think I would be better off as a man in my insurance career."

\*

"Maternity leave held me back from being a director of a clinic."

\*

"Only one woman in my current employer holds a senior executive position."

## MANY PARTICIPANTS RAN INTO OTHER KINDS OF DISCRIMINATION THAT WOULD NOT DIRECTLY LIMIT MOVEMENT UP THE LADDER OR EARNINGS

It's important for professional women to understand that even though wage and promotion discrimination is fairly low, there are other kinds of discrimination that professional women run into on a more regular basis. Women need to be aware of this discrimination and be prepared to handle it if it occurs. These situations are generally easily handled by women with high self-esteem and good assertive skills.

The number of men who make assumptions or treat women poorly purely because they are women is very small. However, because today's professional women come into contact with such a large number of men (in both their personal and professional lives), most professional women will eventually encounter bigoted men. They range from men who unconsciously believe a subtle generalization about women to those that hold conscious biases about what women are capable of doing or what they should not be doing (such as working in specific fields).

Run-ins with such men can range from the trivial to the critical. While the trivial situations need not always be addressed head on, they do provide a fertile training ground for improving your assertive skills while keeping your emotions in check. However, it is generally imperative that the critical run-ins be addressed quickly. The critical situations have the ability to impact your reputation, your professional goals, and your career.

### My Personal Experiences

#### 1. Car Salesman

I had a trivial run-in with a car salesman when I was fresh out of college. I had saved $5,000 for a used car and had brought my boyfriend Dave (who is now my husband) with me to shop. This particular car salesman kept addressing his questions to Dave. I told him at least three times that I was the one buying the car. Immediately after telling him for the third time that I, not Dave, was buying the car, the salesman turned directly to Dave and asked him, "What color car does she want?" At this point it was almost humorous how thick this car salesman was. We left the dealership. There is no enlightening the extremely thick.

### 2. Speaking Engagement

Another trivial example occurred when I was invited to be a speaker at a seminar of fifty salesmen that was taking place at a golf resort. Everybody attending the seminar received a golf shirt. The sales manager had wanted to mix the group up so he placed the golf shirts containing the attendees' names on yellow stickers throughout the room. I was the only woman at the seminar. As the attendees arrived, they had a difficult time finding their names (places where they were to sit). One of the salesmen came up to me and told me his name and asked me where he was sitting. He just assumed that I was the manager's secretary and therefore should be responsible for such things. I told him I didn't know where he was sitting. When it was my turn to speak, he turned a little red. He later apologized for the false assumption. No big deal.

### 3. Vendor One

I had a critical run-in with two individuals from a Big 5 accounting firm who were bidding on a contract to provide services for my company. To make a long story short, they had bid on a contract that had the potential of being worth a few million dollars. A decision was made to go with one of their competitors for this project. I made the call to let them know. The next day they were meeting with my boss on an unrelated proposal and started bad-mouthing me and asked my boss outright if he could overrule me and get them my contract. He told them it was my contract and immediately called me after his meeting with them was over. To say I was outraged at their unprofessional conduct would be an understatement.

This is one of those tests that comes along every so often out of the blue and shows everyone what you are truly made of. Your reaction to these situations will greatly impact your professional reputation. If you decide to ignore these situations, you could be viewed as a wimp who does not belong in management. If you face it head on in a professional manner, you will more likely be viewed as a qualified professional who is not afraid to step up to the plate when necessary.

I faced it head on and confronted the individuals. A partner from the accounting firm, whom I had worked with on various other projects, let me know that these individuals did not believe that a woman could be empowered to make decisions on such a large contract, and that they thought nothing of trying to bypass me by stepping on my reputation. Their firm has since implemented training to eliminate the chance of repeating this situation.

It is very important to protect your professional reputation. The projects, promotions, and job offers you receive will all be affected by the professional reputation that you develop. Avoid being categorized as a wimp. Wimps have a reputation for not being able to handle "fires," and are therefore not promoted to the higher positions. Stand up for yourself and do not allow others to intentionally walk over you. Always remain calm and professional in handling any such situation. Overreacting or being a drama queen is just as bad as being a wimp. That does not mean that you shouldn't tell someone how angry you are about unprofessional behavior. Moreover, never gossip or discuss these situations. The only people who should be informed are the parties directly involved or others who may have received misinformation about you that could damage your reputation. Beyond that, do not discuss the event unless directly asked about it.

### 4. Vendor Two
I had a conflict with another vendor who treated me poorly just because I was a woman. These men are not going to excel in sales unless they learn not to mistreat the

purchasing decision makers who just happen to be women. My company's transportation department manager called me because a consulting company was trying to sell them on a tax savings idea. The salesman, Terry, had told the manager that he needed copies of our tax returns and some additional financial information in order to

1. determine whether their idea would work for us,
2. to estimate potential savings, and
3. to create a written proposal.

I receive a dozen such calls a week from vendors attempting to sell tax savings ideas; however, this one had what seemed to be a new and fresh idea. I decided that if their idea was legitimate and feasible, if it fit within my company's plans, and if they had the appropriate credentials that checked out, I would give my stamp of approval for providing the summary information they needed to perform their calculations.

Upon asking Terry my first tax question, he gave me a very superficial answer — the type of answer that would only be provided to an individual who knew nothing about taxes. Yet, he knew I was responsible for such taxes. Did he think that I was promoted to the position I held without a tax background?

I decided to ask him a second tax question. In response to my second question, Terry said, "We work with companies much larger than yours." In effect, he was not answering my tax question and was implying that I should just hand over the information they requested without any knowledge of who they were or what they wanted to do with the information. At this point, Terry was sounding very full of himself and was showing a lack of respect towards me.

I asked him whether he understood that I was the gatekeeper of the information that he was requesting. By asking him this, I was trying to nicely tell him that he was beginning to step over the line and was in the process of losing a potential sale. I then asked him to send literature about his company and credentials because I was not going to authorize the release of confidential information to him without knowing anything about him or his company. At this point, he said, "It is clear that you are full of self-importance and I have no time to deal with you." He then hung up without a goodbye. Who was self-important? I was just doing the job I was hired to do. Releasing confidential information without knowledge of what it would be used for, or who it was going to, would have been an inexcusable blunder. I don't believe that Terry would have been so disrespectful had I been a man. But who knows. Maybe he treats everyone this poorly.

In the end, I gave Terry's boss a call. He thanked me for the call. He said he always appreciated feedback about why his company lost specific sales.

## 5. Customer

I had another run-in with a customer who made purchases from my company. One of our managers was having trouble collecting the appropriate state documentation from this customer, so she conferenced me into a call with this customer. As a courtesy to some of our customers who are unfamiliar with the law, we sometimes educate them on why we are legally required to collect certain types of documentation from them. This individual, ignorant of the law, thought I was off the wall. Within the first thirty seconds of the call, he started cursing at me. The word "f_ _ _ing" was my cutting off point. I told him his language was unprofessional, and that I was going to end the conversation. I disconnected him from the call between the manager and myself. About three minutes later, I received a call from my boss stating that this customer called him, admitted to the inappropriate language, and was going to call to apologize to me and the other woman on the phone with us. He did. I do not believe this man would have spoken to me in this manner nor would he have assumed my ignorance on the subject had I been a man. But again who knows. Maybe he treats everyone this poorly.

## EXAMPLES OF OTHER TYPES OF DISCRIMINATION FROM THE STUDY PARTICIPANTS

"I raised a sexual harassment issue, and it was not handled well. The company sent me for counseling. I eventually left the job."

This woman made changes in her career path and believes she would be no further along nor earning anymore today had she been a man. She took her career into her own hands.

*

"I work in the construction industry. I feel that as a woman I have to work harder to prove my value and to gain credibility than men do."

*

"In graduate school, other students told me I received my fellowship because I was a woman. This was extremely difficult for me to handle, and I struggled to maintain my self-confidence."

Otherwise, this woman did not believe she had faced discrimination. This is one of the reasons that quotas and incentives biased towards women are undermining women in the workforce. Women's achievements and credentials are overlooked by those who perceive that women are receiving free rides. Eliminating quotas and incentives will add much more credibility for women competing with men in the free market.

\*

"This isn't really serious discrimination but I have found in previous positions that the men in my same level or position always did 'lunch' together and I was never included or made to feel like part of the team."

This is a true problem, especially when much of the team building or work takes place at lunch. Most men are not trying to keep women down by not inviting them to such events and would actually be happy if their female peers would join them; however, many men feel awkward asking. Women need to pull out that self-esteem and those assertive skills and let it be known that they would like to attend.

\*

"I felt that a potential employer did not hire me because my husband was in the Navy. The potential employer knew we would probably be moving."

\*

"Judges and other attorneys have called me honey, etc. which does not particularly offend me, but might have offended other women."

\*

"I worked for a number of years at a large corporate law firm. I did not experience overt discrimination. However, many of my female colleagues and I felt that young male attorneys received more significant mentoring from senior attorneys (who were mostly male). This mentoring is often essential for success or satisfaction in this career path."

In the end, this woman made a career move and now believes that she would not be any further along in her career, nor would she be earning any more today, had she been a man. She does not believe that discrimination has held her back. Here is another example of a woman who took her career into her own hands.

\*

"At a business meeting at a plush country club, I was the only woman with ten men. When the meeting concluded, most of us realized that I was the only one that had not been invited to play golf. I laughed it off."

This is similar to the lunch scenario. I have found that whenever there has been such an event, I have always seen the men go out of their way to make sure that the women are also asked to golf. I am sure this woman was unintentionally overlooked. Things like this happen. Women need to speak up and be assertive. If you are meeting at a golf club, you need to assume many will be playing golf after the meeting. If you are interested in playing, ask whether anyone plans to play. If they are, let them know that you are interested.

I am a very poor golfer. Whenever I am asked to play, I decline. However, I do not believe that not playing golf has held me back in my career.

\*

"I believe I was treated differently. Confronted supervisor, who denied treating me differently because I am a woman. However, I believe most discrimination is insidious and that people are not aware they are treating women differently."

\*

"I have been pressured to hire minority candidates not qualified for positions. I try to hold off Human Resources long enough to interview qualified personnel and hire the most qualified individuals – black, white, or purple."

This goes back to quotas and incentives. Women do not want anyone saying that they were hired to make the companies diversity figures look better. Women want to be hired because they are the best candidates for the job.

\*

"I was sexually harassed verbally by another attorney at my firm. I simply downplayed the entire conversation and tried never to be alone with him after hours. I basically ignored him."

There were only two participants in the study who encountered sexual harassment. While I am encouraged that only 2% of the population encountered sexual harassment, extrapolating that 2% across the female population of the United States suggests that there are millions of women who face this situation.

When I was at a large corporate cocktail party where a few of the attendees were drinking as if they were back in college, one man said a few words to me. Because I was standing with a large group and the noise in the room was so loud, I had no idea what he said to me — so I just nodded. Later that evening, one of the people who had been standing with me apologized for the other man's comments, indicating that they were way out of line. The next morning, the culprit apologized to me for his outrageous behavior. To this day, I have no idea what he said. Had I known what he said that night, I would have been assertive, and he would not have gotten off so easy. I am sure those other individuals who were standing with me and heard his comments must have thought I was a wimp by not responding (or at least rolling my eyes and walking away).

*

"Although I have never been discriminated against by an employee or co-worker there are a few situations that stand out in my mind as being "problems" that would not be encountered by a male:

    1) I often would receive less respect from outsiders because I was a young woman. When I first started my career at

23 I performed enforcement inspections for the state environmental agency. I would go out to a site with a fellow co-worker (male) who I was training and the site management/personnel would respond to my co-worker even though I was running the inspection and asking the questions. This happened on many occasions.

2) I have had people at work sites, including state employees, call me babe, or some similar form of the word. Although I am sure they did not mean any offense, it demeans me and reduces my respect as an enforcement inspector.

3) I have had a coworker, who at the time was my senior (and whom I was working for/with) make a serious pass at me outside of work hours. You don't need the details, I'm sure, but it was clearly a pass. Groping was involved. He was drunk and, because I am against drunk driving, I gave him a ride home. He apologized the next day but I always felt he was leering at me (especially when he drank). He was clearly aware he was wrong (and I told him) but I have never been comfortable with him since then, and I have left that company."

The above example is inexcusable. Drinking is not a justification for such behavior.

Just as men can make fools of themselves when they drink too much at business events, some women do the same thing. Never drink too much at professional functions. You never want to wake up the next morning embarrassed by something you did or said.

*

"There was no gender discrimination, but I worked for a company where the younger staff members, including myself, were treated differently/ with less respect. We addressed the issue. It was acknowledged that there was a problem and efforts were made to change that."

This is a good example of recognizing a problem, asserting oneself in a professional manner, and achieving a good outcome.

\*

"In working for one of the large public accounting firms, most of the men were given the more interesting and high profile auditing jobs."

\*

"I was denied a position because of my ethnic background. I was the most qualified candidate educationally and professionally, but a person with less education and experience was hired because she was of color."

The woman who wrote this was not a minority.

\*

"I have seen discrimination happen to other women. I was once told not to promote a recently married female because "she'll have kids and leave you for 13 weeks" (our paid maternity leave). I hired her."

## Referring to Women as Girls

One of my pet peeves is being in a professional situation and being called a girl. A girl is defined as a female child. People who use the word girl generally do not intend any disrespect when they use the word. Yet it is disrespectful. Over the long run it can chip away at people's impression of you. For example, in many offices, the women holding clerical positions (such as office assistants, secretaries, and receptionists) are often referred to as "the girls in the office," while the professional women in the office may not be referred to as girls. It does not matter that one of those "girls" is fifty-eight years old. The distinction between being a girl and a woman should not be based upon a woman's degree or the position she holds. This is even more bothersome when a professional woman refers to the secretarial staff in an office as "the girls."

On the first day of a new job, a peer referred to me as a girl. His exact words to the person on the phone with him were, "The new girl just walked into my office." While smiling, I mouthed the words, "I am not a girl." He relayed this information to the person on the phone with him, and he hung up laughing. He had been talking with a woman partner at the firm who thought it was great that I had corrected him. He never referred to me as a girl again.

There are times when it is inappropriate to correct these lesser blunders. I was representing my company at an appeal hearing where I was clearly winning, and the decision maker said, "This girl has made a good point…" Contradicting someone who is about to decide in your favor would be a big faux pas.

Even those known for being politically correct falsely refer to women as girls. When I was testifying at the House Ways and Means Committee Congressional Hearing, I had a Congressman come up to me afterward and comment, "Here is the young girl who surprised us all with her testimony…" Again, I decided it would be inappropriate to correct this Congressman. He was giving me a compliment and had probably referred to women as girls for the past sixty years of his life. Even if I had called his attention to it, I am sure he would still be referring to women as girls the next day.

I am afraid there is a double standard when using the word girl. It's acceptable for women to refer to themselves as girls, such as, "I am going out with the girls tonight," but it is not acceptable for men or women to use it when referring to women in the workplace.

## Discrimination Summary

The study of professional women revealed that the majority of well-educated women do not believe that they have been discriminated against, nor do they expect to encounter discrimination in their future. However, discrimination does exist and professional women need to know what constitutes discrimination and be prepared to handle it if it occurs. Keeping a level head, remaining professional at all times, and possessing the necessary self-esteem and assertive skills are essential to properly confronting discrimination.

Devorah Gilbert, a Radcliffe economics graduate, put her assertive skills to good use early in her career when she was employed as a strategic planner at CBS. During a meeting of CBS senior executives, she was asked by a recording industry executive: *"Voulez-vous couchez avec moi?"* Translation: "Will you go to bed with me?" She told him off and from that point on had the reputation for being able to handle tough situations. She gained the respect of the offending executive who later tried to recruit her based on the working relationship that was established after this incident.

There is a pattern in the participants' lives after facing discrimination. Those who faced it head on and did something about it generally believe that they are not earning any less today and do not believe they would be any farther along in their careers today had they been men. The women who encountered discrimination and just accepted it generally believe they are earning less today and are not as far along in their careers due to the discrimination.

The statistics that "women earn 75¢ for every dollar earned by a man" and "women only hold 10% of the senior management positions at Fortune 500 Companies" are misleading. Most of the discrepancies found between the wages and positions held by men and women are due to factors unrelated to discrimination. Hours worked, past work experience, education, profession chosen, and the other choices women make to obtain and maintain family-friendly positions are not factors related to discrimination.

Of the women studied who believe discrimination against them as women has impacted their earnings, the majority of them base that belief solely on statistics that say "women make less than men," and not on any true knowledge of wage discrimination. Because the majority of the wage gap is not due to discrimination, but is due to other factors, these women have been misled into believing they make less because of discrimination. Women need to know what they are worth by conducting research and interviewing to avoid jumping to false conclusions.

A question for thought. If economic conditions in the United States plummet and unemployment increases, do you believe that the strides women have made in the workplace will be lost?

# CHAPTER 7

# Planning &
# Following Through

Once you have prioritized your goals and have evaluated whether they can be met in spite of the limitations that will be placed upon them, it's time to create a work plan to meet those goals. The work plan will consist of a detailed time line for achieving your aspirations.

For example, assume you are twenty-one years old, you hold a degree in teaching, and your goals include:

- studying for the teacher's exam and becoming licensed in your state,
- obtaining a teaching position,
- attending night and weekend classes to achieve

a graduate degree in special education,
- obtaining a position in special education, and
- having your first child before you are age thirty-two.

You may create the following time line:

At age twenty-one,
- pass the teachers exam and become licensed in the state,
- write a great cover letter and resume,
- send it out for all positions that interest you, and eventually
- start working as a teacher.

At age twenty-two,
- save money for graduate school while you work,
- research the schools in your area that offer programs that you are interested in, and
- apply to the schools that meet your requirements (reputation, cost, class times, close to home, etc.).

Between the ages of twenty-three and twenty-seven, earn your degree by taking classes at night or on weekends.

At age twenty-eight,
- write another great cover letter and resume,
- send it out for all positions that interest you, and eventually
- start working in your specialty.

Between the ages of twenty-nine and thirty-two, start trying to conceive a child.

This time line is very reasonable. The chance of achieving and sticking with it are very good. However, unforeseen future events and obstacles may influence whether it can and will be achieved. For example, once you begin teaching, you may decide that teaching is not for you, and you may forego earning a degree in special education for a position in sales. Or by the time you are thirty-two, you may not have met your husband.

Once you have created your plan, you will need to reevaluate it on a regular basis. Take advantage of the opportunities that arise and make your own opportunities where you can. When reevaluating your work plan, you need to ask yourself a few questions:

- Did you meet your expectations for the current year?
- Have any of your highest expectations or goals changed?
- Are the resources still available to meet these goals?

## Obtaining a New Job

*Finding a new job needs to be attacked as a job in itself.* Too many people shortchange themselves by not doing enough when they are looking for a job. Many people create mediocre resumes, apply for just a few positions, are not prepared for interviews, and accept the first position that they are offered.

Doing too little in the search for a new position is the main reason why many people

- earn less than they otherwise could earn,
- work at companies with poor corporate cultures,
- do not receive benefits that are offered at other companies (such as tuition reimbursement), and

- work at companies with fewer opportunities for promotion (have bottle gaps in reaching upper positions).

Do not shortchange yourself. Gear up for finding a new job and invest the time to do it right. This is your future. Don't compromise.

## 1. RESEARCH HOW MUCH OTHERS IN YOUR PROFESSION ARE EARNING

Begin your quest by rereading the section of this book titled "What are others in your profession earning?" It appears under the section titled "Money" in Chapter 4, on page 50. Do not enter the race without knowing what others are earning.

## 2. WRITE A PRELIMINARY RESUME

Go to the library or a bookstore and read their current books on resumes and cover letters. Look for resume examples in similar fields. Then write a preliminary resume and cover letter.

Use a computer with a word processing program to write your preliminary resume and cover letter. Later, you will tailor each resume to the specific position that you are applying for and each cover letter to the specific circumstances under which you are applying (response to an advertisement, cold call, referral from a friend, etc.).

## 3. LOCATE THE JOB OPENINGS

The next step is to locate the job openings. Try all avenues. Research job listings on the Internet and in the newspapers. Many larger newspapers now list their classified sections on the Web. Here are a few places to begin your search:

- www.monster.com
- www.careermag.com
- www.cweb.com
- www.joboptions.com
- www.recruitersonline.com is a good place to start when you are in a niche profession; however, as discussed later, avoid using recruiters when possible.

New Internet job sites are being added daily. Do your homework and surf the Web. Friends, mentors, and networking can also provide leads to companies with job openings.

Many individuals want to work for specific companies (such as those viewed as: being prestigious, having great growth potential, specializing in a particular industry, having great benefits, being female-friendly, etc.). If you want to create such a list, a good place to start is with the following annual articles:

- *Working Woman* magazine's list of the top twenty-five companies for executive women,
- *Working Mother* magazine's list of the one hundred best companies for working mothers, and
- *Fortune* magazine's list of the one hundred best companies to work for.

However, do not fall under the misconception that these are utopian companies where all employees love working. You still need to do your homework. I have a friend who works for one of the companies listed by *Working Mother* magazine as the one hundred best companies for working mothers. Everything they wrote in the article on her company is true, however they missed one important point. As a mother, she is still expected to work more than sixty hours per week. This drowns out all the other perks that she receives.

If you have a list of companies that you would like to work for, and you haven't seen any openings for your specific position at those companies, call the heads of the departments where you want to work (skip calling the HR departments). If you do not know the name of the department head, ask the receptionist. If she does not know, ask her to put you through to the secretary in that area, and then ask the secretary who is the head of that department.

Once you reach the department head, tell her a little bit about yourself (degree and background in two sentences), and that you are interested in working for her company in her department. Then ask whether they are or may be looking for such a person in the near future. You would be surprised how many companies have departments that need to be staffed up and would gladly hire an extra person, but that information never hits their human resources department because the understaffed departments are just too busy to start the process. If they are looking, or may be, offer to send your resume.

When making cold calls, be aware that you may often hear that they are not currently looking for anyone. Do not let this get you down. Keep trying, it only takes one.

I recommend avoiding headhunters and recruiters when possible. Generally, these individuals are paid by the company with the job opening when they find the candidate that is hired. Their fee is normally based on a percentage of your first year's salary. This is money that otherwise could be in your pocket if you found the job yourself and were good at negotiating. Often, companies will use recruiters and will advertise the position themselves. Hold off on going the recruiter route at first, you may stumble across the position yourself. Wouldn't you rather negotiate a salary that is $3,000 more a year, than see a recruiter paid $5,000 for finding you?

The problem is that classified advertisements written by recruiters often do not state that they are recruiters. For example, one advertisement may be seeking a professional to fill a management position at a Fortune 500 Company. This advertisement may have been written by a company that wants to remain anonymous, or it may have been written by a recruiter.

If the advertisement provides a phone number, calling the number and asking a few basic questions about the position should reveal whether it is a recruiter or the company that you are calling. If you are unsure, you can always ask. Be aware that there are some recruiters with reputations similar to those of the sleaziest car salesmen. It's best to stay away from these individuals. At the same time, there are many reputable recruiters who provide a very valuable service to companies that need employees and do not have the time to look for recruits themselves. There are a few positions that are only offered through recruiters.

If there is no phone number and no company name located in the advertisement, you should be able to perform a reverse look-up to find the name of the company at that address. Everyone knows how to find phone numbers. A reverse look-up is where you either know the phone number or the address and you want the name of the individual or company. Many people already have access to this service via their Internet provider or their phone company. The free Web site that has worked best for me is www.teldir.com/eng. Once you click on "United States," you have the option of searching by address or phone number. They then put you right into AT&T's AnyWho or InfoSpace's reverse locators.

## 4. REWRITE YOUR RESUME FOR THE SPECIFIC POSITION THAT YOU ARE TARGETING

Once you have decided to apply for a specific position, rewrite your resume emphasizing your past experiences and achievements that are most in line with what the company is looking for. We all wear various hats in the positions that we hold. Different hats will be important to different employers. You need to emphasize the hats that most persuasively show that you have the experience and background necessary for the position for which you are applying.

## 5. GET READY FOR THE INTERVIEW

The next step is to read books on interviewing. One of the best is *Best Answers to the 201 Most Frequently Asked Interview Questions* by Mathew J. DeLuca. The best way to prepare for an interview is to read his book and prepare your answers to the tougher questions.

Next research the company. What has their stock been doing over the last few years? What do the analysts say about the company's outlook and growth potential? Have their been any news releases regarding this company?

In most professions, your appearance will not carry the same weight as your resume or your answers to interview questions in obtaining a job; however, even if you have the winning resume and answers, a poor appearance can sabotage your chance to obtain the position.

The most important characteristic in your appearance is the portrayal of your self-esteem. If you come off as being self-confident, and you do not appear weak or wimpy, you are much more likely to get the job over someone with similar credentials who appears meek. You cannot expect others to believe in you, if you are not portraying a positive belief in yourself. Do not appear shy or intimidated by the interviewer.

If you do not have self-confidence, you should strive to project it anyway. Make eye contact, sit up straight with your shoulders back, and whatever you do, sit still. I remember interviewing a fidgeter. He may not have been on drugs, but he was sure out of control. It's also very important that you are positive in your affirmations that you can handle the job and that you are excited about it. Having self-confidence does not mean that you have to act like a man or lose your feminine characteristics. Being feminine, however, does not mean being sexy, sleazy, or flirtatious.

Do not go into the interview worrying about whether you will get the job. Worrying will undermine your confidence. Every top executive has at sometime in his career received rejections. We all go through it. Expect to receive some rejections. If you haven't yet received a few rejections, then you are not interviewing for the tougher positions or have not sent out enough resumes.

Another appearance characteristic is the superficial items such as your clothes, hairstyle, and jewelry. In many companies, if you do not fit their idea of what an employee should look like and how an employee should dress, you are out. I know it's very superficial, but that's the way it is with some companies. However, if you are a person who is not interested in wearing suits and appeasing the dress code god, then take heart — you have been born at the right time. Many companies are now much more excited about hiring individuals with enormous talent and potential over individuals who are willing to bend to a dress code memo.

The field that you have chosen will dictate what percentage of companies will be more lax on dress. If you are in the computer field and applying to one of the newer companies, the dress code is likely to be very informal. If you are a teacher, the dress code will be a little stricter. If you are an attorney, suits will probably be a must. Of course, if you work for yourself, you can create your own dress code.

When dressing for an interview, always dress one step above what is required. First appearances always remain with people.

Personally, I do not mind dressing up when I have to go into the office. Since I am in a home office setting most of the time (very lax dress code), it's a nice change. But the main reason I dress up when I am meeting with others professionally is that I am taken more seriously when I am dressed up. It may have to do with being petite or looking young (well, at least I used to look younger than my age). But for whatever reason, when I am professionally dressed, I am taken much more seriously.

Now there are many career counselors who will try to tell you that there are certain standards you must abide by when interviewing, such as wearing dark suits, never wearing slacks, and keeping the heels fairly low. I am afraid these individuals have led a very sheltered life. There is nothing wrong with adding some personality and color to your wardrobe (depending upon whom you are interviewing with and your profession). An intelligent woman does not need to be told how to dress. Just use common sense.

In the past, I have heard from several women that, in their companies, women who wear slacks cannot make it up the corporate ladder. Then along comes an intelligent, self-confident woman with ambition who is promoted, although she wears pantsuits.

Whether you are dressed up or casual for your job, women's clothes cost more. When my husband and I shop together, he often suffers from sticker shock. A woman's sweater that is very similar to a man's sweater in the same department store can often cost three times as much. So when you purchase an interview outfit, you need to think of it as an investment. You have already spent thousands on your education. Are you willing to take a chance of losing a job to someone with the same experience and credentials who was willing to spend a little more on appearance? Spend the money to get an outfit that will complement your education and credentials, not detract from them.

Again, this is less important in certain fields where dress is not as important.

If dress is important in your company and you want to move up, dress for the next position that you want to hold in your company. If you do not, your choice of clothes could prevent you from attaining that next position. Again it's superficial, but that's the way it is at some companies. Know your company's attitude.

The higher you move up the ladder and the busier you become with family obligations, the more superficial appearance items go out the window. The first one is generally the nails. Have you noticed that the higher a woman's education and the higher up the ladder she goes, the less likely that she has her nails manicured on a regular basis? Of course, women in certain industries (such as fashion) are more meticulous about such details. It does not matter if your nails are done or not, as long as they don't detract from a clean professional look. If you like your nails manicured, do it. Just don't let the unessential details worry you too much. The same thing goes for makeup and hairstyles. As long as you don't look twenty years out of date, knowing the latest fads for makeup and hairstyles is not as important as having a clean professional look.

## 6. KEEPING TRACK/EVALUATING OFFERS

Keep track of all the work you are doing to obtain a job. Keep copies of all cover letters and resumes that you send out, along with copies of the job advertisements. Also keep track of who you interviewed with, rejection letters, and calls that you have received. After a reasonable length of time (one or two weeks), follow-up on resumes and interviews with companies you have not heard back from.

On the offers that you do receive, do not assume that the amount offered is as high as they will go. There is generally room for negotiation on salary, vacation, and other benefits.

Companies that make you an offer often want your answer within a very short time. Do not settle for a position because a company tells you that you must decide right away. Generally, the company took time to respond to your resume, set up the interview, and finally make the offer. If it took them two weeks to make up their minds, it is reasonable that you should be able to take two weeks to make up yours. Of course, if they have a second candidate, and they believe you are going to decline the position, you may want to speed up your decision so that you don't lose the position.

The fact that most companies want quick responses to job offers is the main reason why your job search needs to be orchestrated quickly. First, determine all of the positions that you will be applying for. Second, send out all of your resumes the same week. If you drag your search out over several months, you may receive and accept a mediocre offer, never knowing that another company you would have sent a resume to down the line would have been willing to pay you twice as much.

Your job search will feel like a quick dash (similar to studying for finals). There is a lot to do in a short period of time. This way, the offers should come in about the same time. Another advantage to this flurry of job searching activity is that when you receive all of the offers at about the same time, you have more room to use them for negotiating a better deal with the company that you really want to work for.

When evaluating the offers, evaluate the entire package, including benefits, pension plan, options, relocation package, and your chances for promotion. Also evaluate whether you will enjoy the job and the people you will be working with (your boss, peers, and employees). Ask why the person who previously filled the position left. If you have concerns, ask whether they would mind you contacting the person who previously held the position. Very few people do this, yet it is the best source of information for evaluating the position. If the person who previously held the position was promoted within the company, that's a good sign that there is upward mobility within the company (assuming he wasn't in the position that you are being offered for twenty years before being promoted). If the person who previously held the position left to join another company, you can reasonably expect to hear something negative about the position or company. Evaluate the information that you receive with a grain of salt. What someone else views as a major problem may be an obstacle that you can quickly overcome.

## 7. PETER PRINCIPLE

The Peter Principle suggests that people often obtain positions that are above their heads.

If you are unsure of whether you can handle a position, apply for it anyway. We often rise and overcome situations that we are insecure about. Insecurity and fear result in over-preparation. Once you are over-prepared (even if you don't know it), you are ready. There is nothing wrong with trying. Even if you fail, it will be a great learning experience.

We have a friend who interviewed for a position that was above her current knowledge base. It paid $60,000, whereas her previous job paid $30,000. She had the credentials for all but one of the areas that the position was responsible for. My husband and I tutored her in that area to prepare her for the interview. When it came to questions about this area, she answered honestly that she didn't have much experience working in that area, but she knew all of the essentials of the area to get the job done. She then rattled off what we had taught her. She got the job. She then read everything she could get her hands on that addressed the subject before she started the job. She never missed a step. The moral of the story is: Invest the time and money to get the job you want. Then you can worry about what you have to do to meet and surpass the expectations for that position. Often, ambitious people will more than excel in positions that were once above their heads.

Of course, there is a chance that the Peter Principal could come back to haunt you. You will have to decide whether it is worth it.

# CHAPTER 8

# Making Compromises & Sacrifices

While working to achieve your highest expectations, you will find that you are having to make compromises and sacrifices in areas that you didn't expect. If you find that the compromises and sacrifices that you are making outweigh the goals that you are striving for, reevaluate your expectations.

Of course there will be compromises and sacrifices that you are willing to make in order to achieve many of your goals.

One of the sacrifices that I have made to balance home, work, and writing this book simultaneously has been to give up putting on makeup when I work out of the home office. I use the time I would have used for putting on makeup to play with my daughter and to write.

Another sacrifice I have made so that I could work on this book has been to let go of all the time-consuming activities that I would normally do late in the evening and on the weekends. For example, we moved into this house several years ago. I have yet to find any special knickknacks for the end tables or pictures to hang on the walls. It takes time to find the right ones. For the last few years, finishing this book was more important than going shopping. However, if this book was scheduled to take me another three years to complete, I would probably decide to take the time for shopping.

I have friends who live in a small row home in the city so that the wife can continue to attend night school to become a nurse practitioner. The sacrifice of living in a smaller house than they could afford, in a location that they are not too thrilled with, is outweighed by the goal of attaining the career.

You will find that many sacrifices and compromises are acceptable over a short, definite period of time; however, goals that require long-term sacrifices without an end in sight are much tougher.

# PART II

# Additional Things
# You Need To Know

# CHAPTER 9

# Women in Management

## Women Bosses

There is a belief held by *some* individuals, that in general, women bosses are more likely to be difficult to deal with, tougher to please, and more irrational than male bosses. I have met old men, young men, old women, and young women who believe there is a disproportionate number of female bosses who fit this stereotype. Fortunately, the individuals who hold this belief are in the minority. However, since this is a theory that you will probably hear at some point in time, you need to be acquainted with it.

All of the foremost hypotheses about how the theory of the stereotypical female boss developed begin with the fact that in the past discrimination against women in the workplace was extremely high. However, the theories part after this basic fact. The three main theories state that when discrimination against women in the workforce was higher,

1. only the tough women were able to break through the glass ceilings. These tough women had similar attitudes and characteristics that made them trailblazers. Yet, many of the attitudes and characteristics that led them to achieve their positions conflicted with the characteristics often found among good managers.

2. there weren't any female role models for women in the workplace to follow. Ambitious women were told that if they wanted to make it, they had to imitate men and hide their female characteristics. This theory believes that these women took that advice to an extreme.

3. men who were biased against working for female supervisors either consciously or unconsciously created this stereotypical depiction of the female boss.

No matter where the stereotype of the typical female boss came from, there are people who still hold this view today. Of the young men and women I have interviewed who believe women bosses are more likely to be difficult to deal with, tougher to please, and more irrational than male bosses, most believe that this is the case only because many older women managers had to be tougher (theory 1) or imitated men (theory 2) to obtain their positions. In general, they do not believe that the younger female managers coming up through the ranks today fit that stereotype.

However, this is still a very hotly debated and controversial topic. In the April 14, 1997 issue of *Fortune* magazine, Anne Fisher addressed this subject in her column "Ask Annie." In that article, she questioned whether female bosses were held to higher standards because women bosses were expected to possess stereotypical female characteristics, such as nurturing. Since that article appeared, she has received an overwhelming response from individuals who provided her with examples of poor female bosses.

Sometime during your career, you may run into female bosses who are difficult to deal with, tough to please, and irrational. This does not mean that there are more female than male bosses who possess these characteristics. Keep an open mind.

On the other hand, as a female, you may encounter bosses, peers, and employees that will be prejudiced towards female managers because they expect women to meet this stereotype until proven otherwise. The best way to change the minds of these biased individuals is to be the best that you can be.

Being a bitch is not a prerequisite or a qualification for moving up. On the contrary, women who believe they must be bitchy to get ahead will become unhappy individuals and will limit what they can achieve. Good companies filter out these bad managers. Managers with bad attitudes corrupt the good working atmosphere that companies work so hard to create. However, "not being a bitch" does not mean that you should give up being assertive. Being a bitch and being assertive are two different things. It's extremely important to be assertive.

If you've watched too many episodes of Melrose Place (or any other soap opera), and you believe it reflects real life, you are out to lunch. The depiction of the power-hungry bitchy female who wears the five-inch skirts and who has affairs with every coworker eventually reaching a powerful position is absurd.

# Mentors & Networking

The picture of what mentoring is has significantly changed over the last decade. The old notion was that young ambitious individuals should latch onto one powerful role model who could open doors for them. The ideal situation was supposedly when a mentor adopted a newcomer and took him under his wing.

This is no longer the ideal mentoring situation. First of all, no one person embodies all of the aspirations and goals that you have set for yourself. Second, people simply do not have the time to provide that kind of mentoring anymore. Third, people move from company to company fairly quickly today. Fourth, mentors often grow tired and bored of individuals who cannot do anything on their own and do not take any initiative.

Today's perfect mentoring scenario is much more complex. It involves surrounding yourself with good people — people who embody the characteristics, attitudes, traits, knowledge, ethics, style, composure, and skills that you would like to replicate in your personal and professional life. Each person need not exemplify all of the things that you would like to copy or become. They need only possess one capacity that you would like to learn or imitate.

Very few individuals possess such outstanding qualities that they deserve your admiration to the point of being raised to mentor status. You cannot just assume that you are going to wake up today and find a mentor who will possess a specific characteristic. You will only run into a few of these individuals throughout your life. It's a matter of recognizing them.

Mentors need not be told that they are your mentors. Often, it is best to keep the relationship with the mentor at the friendship level. When someone finds out that they are a mentor, it often puts undo pressure on that person to live up to your admiration. In a give-and-take friendship, there is often an unspoken admiration that goes both ways.

Depending upon the quality that deserves to be emulated, mentors need not be of the same sex or race as you. Many men possess great qualities. Do not limit yourself by only socializing (surrounding yourself) with other women. If you do that, you'll be overlooking the great male role models who cross your path.

You do not need to know all of your mentors personally. If there is a person who deserves your admiration, you need not have personal contact with that person in order to duplicate her positive qualities.

There are four individuals who I consider my mentors. Not one of them knows it, nor needs to know. All are friends I greatly admire. My first role model is one of the top individuals in my field. If I could, I would download his technical knowledge into my brain. My second mentor is a role model for being a great manager. She always handles situations in a professional manner and motivates everyone around her to do what is necessary and right. My third mentor is a role model for focusing on what is really important in life. My fourth mentor inspires and motivates me to think outside the box.

Beyond identifying mentors that you greatly admire, you also need to surround yourself with other good individuals. These need not be individuals that you greatly admire (like your mentors), but people that you enjoy being with, who bring something special to the friendship. They can

- be role models,
- be from other companies or departments,
- be in higher or lower positions than you,
- have an intimate knowledge about your company's internal politics,

- be willing to share their mistakes,
- be individuals who stimulate you, or
- individuals who have answers to your questions.

However, make sure that the individuals you associate with do not have negative aspects that outweigh their positive qualities. Bad qualities are sometimes contagious, such as gossiping or having a bad attitude. In addition, others may assume that you possess the bad characteristics of the individuals you associate with. It's an old saying, but it still holds true: If you lay down with dogs, you may get up with fleas. Raise yourself up by surrounding yourself with good people. Good people come in all colors and occupations. Do not limit yourself by being a snob. The mail clerk in your company may have many great qualities that would make him a better friend and role model than an individual on the fast track to nowhere.

Recently, some very large companies have been assigning higher level employees to be mentors of lower level employees. These programs have received a lot of media attention and have been touted as great for those involved. When interviewing participants of these programs however, I have not heard many positive comments.

A true mentor cannot be assigned. Imagine going into work tomorrow and being told, "This is Stephanie. From now on she is going to be your mentor."

Choosing a mentor is a very personal decision. Except for the mentors you admire from afar (that you do not know personally), there must be a relationship with the person before they are raised to mentor status. The bonds and admiration should grow naturally. It cannot be forced. If the only criteria for a good mentor was that the person was a female who had achieved a position above yours, good mentors would be a dime a dozen. Choose your mentors wisely. The very good ones worth emulating do not come along often.

Many of the companies that have established mentoring programs have underlying motives that will not be in line with your own motives. Several companies have found that assigning a higher employee to a lower employee reduces training costs and provides easily accessible information about the progress and potential of the lower employee — neither of which establishes an honest basis for a solid mentoring relationship. Both goals, however, make good business sense, but they should not be disguised as mentoring programs. Do not be fooled into thinking that you are being assigned your next best friend. It does not usually work that way.

Companies that want to promote the development of true mentoring relationships should provide informal events where interaction between employees from various departments and from various levels is natural, not forced.

Part of the process of surrounding yourself with good people includes networking. This can take place through friends, associates, organizations, and acquaintances. Again, networking relationships cannot be forced. It's a matter of finding opportunities to meet good people. The more people you meet, the more people you will find that inspire you. Networking can yield new friends, contacts, information, and resources.

As with public speaking, people fear networking. That fear often turns into avoidance. Many great networking opportunities are wasted because individuals feel insecure in these settings. Attendees at such functions often associate with the individuals they know, rather than introducing themselves to those they don't. Do not rely solely on individuals you know to introduce you to others at such functions. They may not know the other attendees, or they may not want to spend their time introducing you to those they do know.

You will need your self-esteem and assertive skills to master networking. Socializing with strangers while appearing to be at ease is very hard. It is that much tougher when the event and the attendees do not interest you. When possible, avoid functions that are likely to bore you. Of course, this is not always possible. It's much easier to network when you truly have interest in the subject and the people attending.

Begin to improve your networking skills by jumping right in. Put yourself in situations where you will be forced to socialize with strangers. As you attend more and more of these functions, you will become more comfortable with socializing with strangers.

Keep in mind that mentoring and networking are no longer about "fitting in." Your goal should be to find the ideal path for you. Surrounding yourself with mentors and good role models is integral to designing the career and personal life that you want for yourself.

## Hormones

It's a fact, women and men are physically different. This does not make one sex better or worse than the other, just different. The physical differences between men and women have very little to do with the quality and type of work performed by professionals.

The word for the physical difference used most often to negatively describe female behavior is "hormonal." Contrary to the belief held by some, most women do not experience hormonal imbalances that make them act in irrational ways. Women are no more irrational than men. However, an outburst from a woman is more likely to be attributed to hormones, while an outburst from a man is more likely to be attributed to having a bad day. Unprofessional outbursts are not acceptable, no matter what the reason. Nonetheless, a woman's outburst attributed to hormones is more likely to negatively impact a woman's reputation than a man's outburst that is chalked up to a bad day. Harnessing emotions in the workplace is essential. You can always scream your lungs out in the car on the way home.

Pregnancy is another area where conduct is attributed to hormonal changes. Again, many women fly through pregnancy without any mood swings. I am not one of them. Mine usually come in the form of crying during commercials (really stupid commercials) and having a shorter fuse in the evenings. Since, I am not in the advertising industry (I don't watch commercials at work), and only my family has to deal with me in the evenings when I am exhausted, my pregnancy-related mood swings do not affect my work.

I have a friend who had a little outburst at home during her last pregnancy. When she discovered that she had severely burnt her grilled cheese sandwich, she became so overwhelmed that she threw the pan in one direction, the sandwich in the other direction, and then sat on the floor for a few minutes crying while she got it out of her system. While no reasonable husband would hold this against his wife, I am sure that if it had happened at work, no one would have forgotten it. Nonetheless, all professionals conduct themselves according to a higher standard at work than they do at home. It is doubtful that she would have allowed such a sight to take place at work. For this reason, it is unrealistic to believe that women act any differently at work when they are pregnant than they otherwise normally act.

That said, if you are experiencing mood swings (whether hormonal or stress related) that you are having trouble controlling, speak with a professional. There is a lot of help out there.

# CHAPTER 10

# Protecting Your Reputation

The most important item that a professional has is her reputation. A good professional reputation is created over time through actions and deeds. Nonetheless, a reputation can easily be diminished to ashes in an instant.

Guarding your reputation is your responsibility. Situations will arise that will have the potential to ding your reputation. You need to know how to avoid these situations when possible, as well as how to defend and respond to attacks.

In your professional life, perception is much more important than truth. How someone perceives you will affect your assignments, raises, and promotions (essentially your professional future). Perceptions can be based on the true you and the true facts or based upon false notions. An individual's perception of you (your reputation) is truth to him whether it is based upon true facts or not.

# Gossip: Avoid Situations Where Someone Could Easily Jump to a Misconception

Gossip is the number one damaging factor to a good reputation. The first step is to avoid situations where someone could easily jump to a misconception. Gossip generally feeds on misconceptions. If you don't give the gossips fodder, they won't have anything to work with.

## PERCEIVED AFFAIRS

The number one issue gossips like to talk about is the perceived affairs (one or both parties being married) going on between employees. I have *never* known of any workplace affairs between employees at the places where I have worked; however, the lack of affairs has never stopped the gossips from talking about them.

The tale I've heard most often about women who have made it into upper management positions is that they achieved those positions only because they had had affairs with their bosses. The top female executives at my first two jobs were both talked about in this way. The rumors undermined the respect they deserved and the support they received from some employees.

Generally, these tales are created when two factors exist. First, a male and female employee have a good casual and natural working relationship. Second, these two individuals are required to spend a lot of time together because of what they are working on. When people spend that much time together, it's only natural that they eat some meals together. They may even be required to travel together. This is what gossips thrive on, and this is where you are going to have to lay your line of defense. What I am going to suggest will sound extremely old-fashioned, but it is the first (and often only) line of defense against such gossip. When the above two situations exist with a male associate, ask a third party to join you to eat when feasible. It's that easy. It does not matter whether the third party is female or male.

Today's men have to protect their reputations, just like women do. Therefore, most men are not going to be averse to having someone else join you. It's not a matter of either party worrying that an affair would occur. It's purely to avoid the appearance. Of course, if you cannot dig up a third party, don't worry about it. You are professionals, and if the gossips cannot handle professional relationships, there isn't much more you can do.

## PERCEIVED EASY WOMEN

The second issue gossips like to talk about is loose female employees. Again, there does not have to be any factual basis for a rumor to start. Generally, these rumors begin with just a slight suggestion. They often are based on the sexy clothing that a woman wears or a flirtatious personality. Not wearing sexy clothes to work and keeping a flirtatious personality under control should be sufficient.

## PERCEIVED POOR WORK

Even though gossips would prefer to talk about sex (sex sells), the most damaging rumors are generally based upon the work itself or the lack thereof. For example, assume you have cleared it with your boss to work extra hours during basketball season in order to leave early on Mondays and

Wednesdays to coach your daughter's team. There is a good chance that someone will make a statement to someone else that you are slacking. That's all it takes to start a rumor. If your work is highly visible, or if others know you are working because you need to leave voice mails and E-mails during off-hours, that should be sufficient to stop rumors. If your work is not visible however, you will need to counteract malicious gossip with a little self-promotion. No one is going to discuss the good work and overtime you are doing if they do not know that you are doing it. That does not mean going overboard by talking about how great you are and how much you bring to the table. It would be sufficient to say that you feel lucky to be able to coach your child's team and make up the work in the evenings. It would also be acceptable to add that the project is coming in under budget or earlier than expected.

## Gossip: Confront False Damaging Gossip Head On

As stated earlier, the first step to protecting your reputation against gossip is to avoid situations where gossips can easily jump to misconceptions. The second step to protecting your reputation is to confront false damaging gossip head on.

A slight misrepresentation of you that is innocent at first can quickly snowball into a major incident that could permanently damage your reputation. These misrepresentations need to be dealt with quickly in a professional manner. For the intentional and malicious situations that arise (and they will arise), you will need your self-esteem and your assertive skills to keep your reputation in tact.

As soon as you get wind of the gossip, it's time to act. The problem is that gossip often occurs without the victim knowing about it until it has become a major problem. A friend of mine was placed in this very predicament. A very innocent situation was blown into something it wasn't by a malicious person. When it reached her boss, he called her into his office, and it was almost the end of her career at that company. She stood up to the accusations, outraged as she was, and the meddlesome gossip was told to keep his mouth shut from then on.

In some situations the person who will soon be starting the gossip gives the intended victim an indication of what he is thinking. The sign could be something as small as noticing the individual's tone towards you changing during a conversation. The sign could also be something as clear as a confrontation. If you receive and pick up on any signal, it's best to address the issue with the individual and put an end to it right away. Gossips tend to find specific individuals they prefer to target. If you stop the gossip in his tracks, it's unlikely that you will be his target again. On the other hand, if you are an easy mark, you will be in his sights often.

When people hear repetitive gossip about one person that goes unchallenged, the listeners often begin to believe the gossip. Very few people question the accuracy of gossip when it's being told as "fact." To question such a gossip would generally be equivalent to calling that person a liar. You cannot protect your reputation if you are not willing to mount a defense, and that takes good self-esteem and assertive skills.

## MY EXAMPLE

Here's my personal example of being on the receiving end of malicious back-stabbing talk. I was on a conference call with my boss and another high-ranking individual with my company. The conversation became a little heated because this individual disagreed with a position that my boss and I were taking. He didn't show anger towards my boss, but by the very end of the conversation he had through his tone and through his words questioned my common sense, my integrity, and my honesty. However, he was such a good manipulator of words (a definite spin-doctor) that I didn't realize the extent of what he had said and implied until I was off the phone.

From his reputation as being a gossip, I knew he was just beginning. I assumed I would be able to nip this in the bud by calling him back and letting him know that his tone and the things he stated on the phone had disturbed me. I was trying not to be too confrontational. I just wanted him to know that he couldn't talk to me in such a manner.

He didn't apologize. He did do a little backpeddling by initially stating that he had a lot on his plate and it was just a miscommunication. But the backpeddling stopped very quickly when he then began to upbraid me on the issue. The harsh tone reentered his voice. At that point, he let me know he already discussed (gossiped) the situation with another person whom he said took his side on the issue. He was a very quick gossip. It took him a mere two minutes from the conversation with my boss and me to run to their mutual boss.

At this point I let him know that he either must fix the situation with my boss, and also their boss (and anyone else he may have already spoken with), or I was going to let them both know how unprofessionally he was behaving. At that point, he calmed down a little and said he would speak with both of them and rectify the situation.

He then got back on his high horse (a very competitive person who does not believe he ever does anything wrong) and stated that I should have tried contacting him earlier on the work-related topic. I explained that I only found out about the issue on Thursday evening and I had left him messages on Friday and Monday. He then jumped on me with an extremely angry "I don't like what you are implying. You could have reached me on my cellular phone." Which was ridiculous because I wasn't implying that he was not responsive in returning my calls. I was just trying to get across the fact that I was not trying to avoid him.

I knew I was getting nowhere with him, so I ended the call. Looking back, I have never dealt with such an irrational person in my life. That combined with the fact that he was a gossip and highly placed in the company was a tough blend to stand up to. Even though he said he was going to rectify the situation, I knew there was no way he was going to set the record straight.

The first line of defense, confronting the individual, didn't work in this situation. The second line of defense is to call in the person above you to handle the situation. In this situation, having a great boss who is not a wimp is imperative. It's part of a boss's responsibility to set the records straight when it involves a professional's reputation (unless of course he believes the employee is wrong).

My boss took care of the situation. As I stated earlier, the argument originally became heated because the individual was disagreeing with a position that my boss and I were taking. In the end, all the parties, except for the gossip, agreed that we should go forward with our initial plan and we did. In the end, everything worked out just fine. End of story.

## GOSSIP SUMMARY

Among the women I interviewed, almost all had examples of similar situations where their honesty, credibility, or reputation had been questioned because of gossip. It's acceptable to get angry in such situations, but stay calm, organize your thoughts, and handle the situation in a professional manner.

Before acting, be sure to first ask yourself whether you are overreacting to the situation because you are mad.

The first line of defense is to speak directly with the individual. This usually works. When it does, there is no reason to go any further. Depending upon the situation, an apology from the individual or a sincere change of heart should be sufficient. Of course, as was my case, there are times when you need to go to the next step. Part of a supervisor's responsibility is to handle such situations. Keep this in mind when you are required to handle similar situations.

When the gossip has reached others, or you are enlightening your boss on the issue, do not overdramatize the situation. Just state the facts "as is." And do not personalize the attack against the other individual.

## Self-Inflicted Damage

Next to gossip by others, the leading cause of damage to one's reputation is self-inflicted. One problem that many women (and men) have is that they talk too much, and when they are talking they often forget their common sense. Work is work and should be kept distant from the intimate details of your personal life. That does not mean that you shouldn't become friends with your coworkers. You should. But it does mean that those personal little details that probably shouldn't be told to anyone don't need to be shared with coworkers down the hall. A great example is Monica Lewinski. Why anyone would tell any coworker such intimate details of a relationship is beyond common sense. Some people just like to talk.

# CHAPTER 11

# Stress

By this point in your life, you are already well acquainted with stress. The first step in reducing stress is to acknowledge that stress is internally created. Events, situations, and other individuals do not create or control our stress levels. We control these levels through our internal responses to events, situations, and other people. Individuals who have trouble seeing that their high level of stress is not caused by a specific individual or event, but by their own responses to these items, will have trouble reducing their stress. Stress cannot be managed until it is viewed as something that is under your own control.

The main cause of stress among professional women is taking on way too much. There are four main reasons we do this:

1. We want to do so many things, but there just isn't the time. Yet we often attempt it all anyway.
2. We believe that too many things fall under our responsibility; however, when these items are analyzed, they really do not have to be our responsibility.
3. We do not say no often enough (which comes back to assertiveness).
4. We want too much control over the way things are done. Instead of allowing someone else to take over, we often do it ourselves.

Prioritize and get rid of the nonessential items. It's okay not to do it all. There is no such thing as the perfect woman or the perfect man, so stop trying to be one. Tell yourself over and over again: "I am just fine the way I am. I don't have to try for perfection. I just need to be myself. From now on, I am only going to stress over those items that are really important."

Other than taking on too much, the second leading cause of stress is an internal overreactive response to specific individuals, events, and situations. Worrying or fretting about things that are out of your control and that are truly not as important as you perceive them is a huge waste of time and energy. Stress should be reserved for the truly critical issues, such as when a loved one becomes ill.

As noted earlier, the second chapter in the book *She Who Dares Wins* is dedicated to dealing with stress.[42] Since this book provides a detailed step-by-step guide for

42. Eileen Gillibrand and Jenny Mosley, *She Who Dares Wins* (London: Harper Collins, 1995).

reducing the stress in your life and creating healthier responses to the stress that does occur, I am recommending that you read the chapter dedicated to stress and follow through on the authors' advice.

They provide stress indicator tests for your personal and professional lives. The tests provide you with an overall score and identify the areas where you need improvement. Once you have identified the areas giving you the most trouble, you are then provided with the information to reduce the stress in your life. A few of the topics are

- learning how to recognize and cope with stress,
- making important changes in your lifestyle,
- developing positive relationships,
- taking care of your own needs, and
- maintaining a balanced view of your life.

Completing the tests and exercises and implementing the strategies to make changes in your everyday life will result in less stress and healthier responses to the stress that does occur. However, don't expect results overnight. The exercises take time to complete. Reconditioning your thoughts and changing your natural responses to specific types of events will take time. Again, it will take an investment in yourself.

# CHAPTER 12

# Homemakers
# Going Back To Work

## When To Go Back To Work

When the homemakers who participated in the study were asked about going back to work, they answered as follows:

- 60% plan to go back to work when their youngest child is school-age (between the age of five and seven),
- 7% when their youngest is ten,
- 7% when their youngest is out of high school, and
- 26% have no plans or are unsure of when they will go back to work.

Keep in mind that among all the homemakers who participated in this study, their oldest child was seven years old. Interviews with homemakers older than those in the study (over thirty-five years old), placed the above results in a different light. Many stated that homemakers who plan to return to work after a few years often have their plans change over time.

For example, assume a mother has a four-year-old and a seven-year-old. That mother may currently believe that she'll reenter the workforce when her youngest is six years old. However, by the time her youngest is six, she may be very involved in the school activities of her older child and may want to provide the same type of support for her younger child. In addition, many homemakers find that over time the fear of less income is balanced by the practice of budgeting, and the fear of losing one's identity by not working is fulfilled by things other than work.

This information is not provided to convince you to stay at home longer. It is provided merely to open your eyes to the experiences of some older women who have already come down this path. Many homemakers do go back to work when planned.

If you are looking for the ideal age when your child will be old enough for you to go back to work, I am afraid there aren't any definitive studies that provide a clear-cut answer. You will need to make the decision for yourself based upon your beliefs, your circumstances, and your personal knowledge of what your children need.

## Preparing To Reenter the Job Market

A whopping 60% of the homemakers in the study worry about reentering the job market. These women have worked hard to obtain their degrees, certifications, and licenses in order to excel in their chosen professions. They know they are not going to be in the same place they would have been had they stayed in the workforce. Nonetheless, these women are very interested in putting themselves in the best position for reentering the market in the future. The question is, how should these women go about doing this? The answer will depend on how long they stay at home and on their profession.

If they are interested in reentering the job market, they'll need to stay abreast of the changes that take place in their profession and the technical advances that occur. This can often be accomplished by subscribing to trade journals and keeping in touch with friends in the profession.

If you leave the workforce for more than a few years, instead of jumping directly back into the workforce, take a year to brush up on your skills and knowledge by taking a few courses. Taking the time to invest in yourself shows potential employers that you are very interested in getting back into your career, and that you now have the updated knowledge to jump back in. This investment may also substantially increase your earnings potential, depending upon your profession and how much it changed while you were at home.

# CHAPTER 13

# Pregnancy & Delivery

## *Working While Pregnant*

For many women, working throughout their pregnancy is a piece of cake. For other women inundated with physical complications (including extreme nausea, pregnancy-related diabetes, and extreme exhaustion), working throughout pregnancy can range from being extremely difficult to impossible.

The problem is that you will not know how your body will react to being pregnant until you become pregnant. Of the homemakers who participated in the study, 81% worked through their first pregnancy. If you cannot physically work during your pregnancy, do not think of it as being disgraceful or less than professional. It's just the hand you've been dealt. In the end, having a healthy child is the ultimate goal. If you have to, it's well worth the time you have to take away from your professional career to focus on your pregnancy.

Once you become pregnant, you will need to decide when you are going to tell your employer. The general rule of thumb is to wait until you have been pregnant at least three months before mentioning it to anyone. The predominant reason for waiting three months is that the largest threat of miscarriage occurs during that first trimester. Between 15 and 20% of all pregnancies end in miscarriage (10% for women under thirty and over 50% for women over forty). An estimated 80 to 90% of those miscarriages occur during the first trimester. It's easier to avoid mentioning that you are pregnant, than to have to explain later that you had a miscarriage. Miscarriage is hard to deal with, let alone when you are forced to talk about it.

Depending upon your physical complications, it may be impossible to hide the fact that you are pregnant. For example, nausea is a fact of life for many pregnant women. It can range from light nausea to extreme nausea, and it can hang on for a month or the entire pregnancy. If you have to relieve yourself from a meeting unexpectedly, or if you are constantly munching on crackers, people may begin to wonder whether you are pregnant.

I never had to run out of a meeting, but I came close a few times. I went as far as to prepare my mental escape route to the nearest bathroom. The problem is that for many women the nausea comes on unexpectedly, with no notice. I didn't have that problem with my first pregnancy, but I have encountered it during this one.

I recently took my daughter to the Philadelphia Children's Please Touch Museum. We were having a wonderful time when it hit. There wasn't enough time to ask anyone where the bathroom was, nor did I want to open my mouth for fear of provoking it. I just headed directly for the door. During this pregnancy, I keep a bag in my car for just such occasions. However, I did not make it in this instance. On a busy Philadelphia sidewalk, with my daughter's wrist grasped tightly in my right hand, I was revisited by breakfast. I received many disturbed looks from passersby. Oh well, it's part of being pregnant. I am thankful that it never occurred during a meeting. But it could have.

## Fear of the Unknown

Today, the first birth that a woman attends in person is generally the birth of her own child. You may have watched a video of a delivery or watched edited portions of a birth on TV. You may even hold the unrealistic belief that you know what birth is about because you have watched a few television sitcoms poke fun at it. However, it is very unlikely that you have ever attended an entire birth in person, before the birth of your own child.

This was not always the case. Prior to the twentieth century, women often attended several deliveries (their mothers, sisters, or friends) prior to having their own children. Women would pass down from generation to generation what to expect, how to cope, and past experiences. When the intimate process of having a baby at home was changed to the sterile environment of having a baby in a hospital, something was lost.

The increase in healthy babies and mothers over this same time period is mostly due to the introduction of prenatal care, improved nutrition, improved hygiene, a safer water supply, the introduction of antibiotics, and improved surgical techniques (as needed).

Today's women go into their first pregnancy without the practical experience and knowledge our great-grandmothers had. Because people fear the unknown, women fear their first labor. The best way to combat this fear is to obtain knowledge. If you eliminate the unknowns and prepare for what you have learned, there is very little to fear.

The two most important points I learned during my first pregnancy were:

1. Pregnancy is a very natural process. It is not a medical condition.
2. Women can take control of their pregnancies and deliveries by finding doctors or midwives who meet their needs.

## PREGNANCY IS A VERY NATURAL PROCESS

Most women are capable of carrying and delivering babies on their own, without any medical intervention. Doctors and midwives are there throughout the process to take measurements, perform lab tests, read ultrasounds (sonograms), and to monitor deliveries. Essentially, they are with you throughout pregnancy and delivery to make sure everything is going well. Mother Nature did an amazing job creating women's bodies to nourish babies, provide an environment for growth, and to give birth without any intervention at all.

Pregnancy and delivery is not a medical emergency and should not automatically be treated as such. If an unusual pregnancy-related emergency occurs, only then does it turn into a medical condition.

## WOMEN CAN TAKE CONTROL OF THEIR PREGNANCIES AND DELIVERIES BY FINDING DOCTORS/MIDWIVES WHO MEET THEIR NEEDS

Depending upon what you desire from your doctor or midwife, it may take a lot of investigating to find one who will meet your requirements. However,

- if you would be happy with a health care provider who is part of a practice where any provider from the practice may be called upon to deliver your baby, and
- you plan on using pain relief medication during delivery,

you are like most women in the United States. If this is acceptable to you, you should have an easy time finding a health care provider. All you have to do is find a practice where you feel comfortable with the healthcare providers, which is associated with a hospital that would also meet your requirements (such as having a birthing suite).

On the other hand, if your requirements are more demanding, it may take some investigating to find a doctor or midwife who will provide what you need. I am afraid I fell into that demanding category. Originally, when I began my quest for a doctor or midwife, I did not think my demands were so outrageous; however, I found that most practitioners could not provide what I was looking for. Consequently, my search took months. I was looking for a practitioner who

- would take me on time for appointments (except for emergencies),
- would address my concerns and answer all my questions,
- held similar beliefs to my own on childbirth, and
- essentially would make me feel comfortable.

It does not sound too demanding; however, four things made it nearly impossible to find a practitioner who supported my beliefs. First, I wanted a natural childbirth (no pain medication if possible). Natural childbirth isn't for everyone, but I wanted to give it a shot.

Second, I knew I would need my practitioner's support throughout delivery to make it through it naturally. Surprisingly, most doctors do not show up at the hospital for many hours. They rely on the nurses to call them if there is a problem or to tell them when it is getting close. Therefore, the nurse becomes the main support person to get you through labor — a nurse you've never met before, who has no idea what your beliefs and plans for your birth are. Labor is not the ideal time for updating your support nurse on your beliefs and plans for delivery.

If you are in the majority of women who plan to use pain medication, at most hospitals you will find many great nurses who will assist you through the delivery process. However, if you are planning on a natural delivery, hospital staff nurses often unconsciously sabotage a woman's intent to deliver naturally. There are three main reasons this occurs:

1. The average hospital delivery nurse does not believe that the average woman is mentally capable of delivering naturally. If your support nurse does not have a positive outlook for you delivering naturally, you are almost doomed to fail. During my first pregnancy, my husband and I attended a birthing class at the hospital where I had planned to deliver. While speaking with the delivery nurse after the class, she told us that it was doubtful that I would be able to make it through a natural delivery. Only 1% of the patients from that hospital deliver naturally. She was not the positive "you can do it" support person that I was looking for. I began to look for a new practitioner — one not associated with that hospital.

2. The average hospital delivery nurse does not possess the knowledge or experience to support a natural delivery. The training that most of these nurses

receive on mentally and physically supporting a natural delivery is extremely light. They generally have the same amount of knowledge as someone who has read one good natural childbirth book. In addition, most delivery nurses have never participated in a well-prepared-for natural delivery (from discussing the birth plan with the patient months ahead of time, to seeing the entire labor through from beginning to end). Thankfully, this gap in education is beginning to change at the more progressive nursing schools.

If you plan to deliver naturally, you need to find a practitioner who

- believes in natural childbirth,
- has been specifically trained in natural childbirth, and
- has a proven success record with natural childbirths.

When I found the perfect group of practitioners to meet my needs (the Birth Center located in Bryn Mawr, Pennsylvania), they not only supported natural childbirth, but 85% of their patients succeeded with their plans to deliver naturally. That is a fantastic success rate. In addition, close to 100% of their patients who have another child return to this practice.

3. Hospitals want compliant patients. Ask a delivery nurse who is easier to deal with, the patient on pain medication or the one going natural. The patient delivering without medication requires a lot more work (physical and mental) from the nurse. For a natural delivery to receive the proper support, a nurse should be dedicated to that patient. However, a nurse can cover several patients on pain medication.

The third item that made it difficult for me to find a practitioner was that I wanted pain medication to be available just in case I changed my mind. Many natural childbirth practitioners do not believe in administering pain medication. The location where I delivered was right across the street from the hospital where my practitioner was associated. Had I changed my mind during the delivery process, I could have gone across the street, and my practitioner would have ordered the pain medication needed.

The fourth thing I wanted was to have emergency medical facilities available just in case something went wrong. Even though true childbirth emergencies are rare, there is the possibility that they can occur. Again, it was nice to have the hospital located just across the street in case such an emergency arose.

No matter what your needs are, it will be your responsibility to make sure you find a doctor or midwife who can meet your needs. No one is going to do it for you.

### Many Doctors Don't Value Their Patients' Time

I've dedicated an entire section to this topic because I am outraged at the doctors who waste our time and do not think anything about it. The first two doctors I went to during my pregnancy never saw me on time. They were always a half hour to two hours late for every appointment. I even tried making my appointments first thing in the morning. That didn't even work. One morning I waited over an hour before my doctor even showed up at the office. It would have been acceptable had she been delivering a baby, but she hadn't been. She was just getting a late start. When I went in for my first ultrasound, my husband and I waited for over two hours.

If making patients wait was the exception, there would be no problem; however, it's turning into the norm for many doctors. Tardy doctors coupled with the sheer number of medical appointments required during a pregnancy makes it very tough for any professional woman to continue balancing everything. Many doctors want to see their patients once a month at the beginning of a pregnancy. By the end, it's up to once a week. Between these visits, there are lab and ultrasound appointments. It adds up to a lot of time. Over the nine-month period, women can easily waste forty hours just waiting to see tardy doctors. Your time is important. Find a doctor or midwife who respects you and sees you on time (except for emergencies).

Finding that many doctors do not respect their patients' time is not limited to the obstetrical profession nor to female patients. My husband and I recently went to see his doctor to find out the results of an MRI he had taken the week before. We took time off from work, drove an hour into the city, and waited forty-five minutes to see the doctor. The doctor spent five minutes with us. During those five minutes, he told us that a few days prior to our visit he had found out that they had taken pictures of the wrong area, and that my husband would have to come back for another MRI. There is no reason that the doctor couldn't have done the courteous thing by calling us, rather than having us take time off from work. But he didn't. Then, he sent us a bill for $65. We questioned the bill, and we were told we had to pay it because the doctor had spent his valuable time with us. So his time is valuable and ours is not?

The practice that I finally found during my first pregnancy never made me wait longer than five minutes for an appointment. There are other practices out there that respect your time; however, they are very tough to find.

# *Books about Pregnancy, Labor, Delivery & Parenthood*

As I stated earlier, the best way to combat the fear of pregnancy, labor, delivery, and parenthood is to obtain knowledge. If you eliminate the unknowns and prepare for what you have learned, there is very little to fear.

Here are a few books that I have found enlightening on various subjects. They take various positions on different subjects, and they do not always agree with one another. Obtain the knowledge that makes you comfortable with making decisions. Then, make the best choices for yourself. One woman's path may not be the ideal path for another woman.

### Books on Pregnancy and Childbirth

*Childbirth Choices Today: Everything You Need to Know to Plan a Safe and Rewarding Birth,* and *Mind Over Labor.* I found these two books to be the most informative. Both were written by Carl Jones. However, these books are not for everyone, because they strongly emphasize natural childbirth choices.

*Your Pregnancy Week by Week* by Glade B. Curtis, MD, FACOG. This book explains what a woman can expect from her changing pregnant body over time.

*The Pregnancy Book for Today's Woman* by Howard I. Shapiro, M.D. provides details on the more technical aspects of pregnancy. This is a great source of information for women who like to research issues in more depth.

*The Girlfriends Guide to Pregnancy (or Everything Your Doctor Won't Tell You)* by Vicki Iovine is a humorous look at pregnancy.

*The New Father's Panic Book: Everything a Dad Needs to Know to Welcome His Bundle of Joy* by Gene B. Williams was written specifically for fathers.

The following books discuss natural childbirth alternatives:

*Special Delivery* by Rahima Baldwin Dancy
*Gentle Birth Choices: A Guide to Making Informed Decisions about Birthing Centers, Birth Attendants, Water Birth, Home Birth, and Hospital Births* by Barbara Harper, R.N.

*Active Birth: The New Approach to Giving Birth Naturally* by Janet Balaskas

*Natural Childbirth the Bradley Way* by Susan McCutcheon

*Labor of Love: Mothers Share the Joy of Childbirth* by Judith Zimmer

### Books on Raising Children

*Touchpoints: The Essential Reference of Your Child's Emotional and Behavioral Development* by T. Berry Brazelton, M.D.

*What to Expect the First Year* by Arlene Eisenberg, Heidi E. Murkoff, and Sandee E. Hathaway, B.S.N.

*What to Expect the Toddler Years* by Arlene Eisenberg, Heidi E. Murkoff, and Sandee E. Hathaway, B.S.N.

### Book on Purchasing Items for the Expected Baby

*Baby Bargains* by Denise and Alan Fields is a guide for any expectant parent bewildered by all those baby products on the market.

# Alternatives During Pregnancy

There are a number of pregnancy-related physical nuisances that may or may not occur during your pregnancy. Today, there are several things you can try for relief. The list includes relaxation meditation, massage, yoga, and maternity aerobics. Look into the alternatives that interest you. There is no harm in trying.

During the last three months of my first pregnancy, I had trouble sleeping. I found that listening to relaxation tapes helped. Often, I became so relaxed that I would fall asleep. The tapes that helped me the most were

- *Letting Go of Stress* by Emmett E. Miller, M.D.,
- *The Joy of Meditating* by Salle Merrill Redfield, and
- *Great Expectations* by Emmett E. Miller, M.D. This tape is specifically for pregnant women.

## Selling My Husband on the Idea of Natural Childbirth

Once I had completed my research and had decided which practice would meet my needs, my next big obstacle was to sell my husband. Since he would be an essential part of the team, it was very important that he was comfortable with my decision to deviate from the standard delivery path.

There were three items I needed to sell him on:

1. A midwife was just as good as a doctor for delivering low-risk babies;
2. a birth center was an acceptable alternative to a hospital setting; and
3. I was going to be able to make it through delivery without pain medications.

The first was an easy sell. Once he learned

- that a midwife was a nurse with extra training, specializing in women's health care (including labor and delivery), and

- the credentials, experience, and delivery statistics of this practice of midwives,

he was comfortable.

The second was a tougher sell. Television inundates the public with the picture that people need to react to a woman in labor as an emergency situation where a woman needs to be in a hospital. Labor is actually a very long process of events that needs to be watched by a trained professional.

The idea that it's an emergency comes from the movies, sitcoms, and other television shows that show panicked husbands racing their wives off to hospitals with their first contraction. The idea is then reinforced by the news shows. When there is a report on labor and delivery, it generally shows a woman who experienced problems during her delivery. However, these shows never provide the actual statistics about how many deliveries actually turn into medical emergencies. Therefore, the viewers assume that deliveries are medical emergencies for all healthy low-risk women. In fact, the opposite is true.

It helped that my husband was impressed with the Birth Center's facilities. The practice is located in an old Victorian home. The entire second floor is for seeing patients, and the first floor is dedicated to a woman in labor. The first floor consists of a family room, a full-sized kitchen, two full baths with Jacuzzis, and two bedrooms with full-sized beds (not hospital beds). It's not brand new, but it is a very warm and inviting private setting.

Any woman planning on natural childbirth, regardless of method, is going to need to be able to fully concentrate on the labor. Limiting unnecessary distractions is essential for natural childbirth. Hospitals are filled with nuisances and distractions for the delivering mother. They range from the hospital's admissions program (which often takes place through the emergency ward) through strange hospital personnel walking into your hospital room on a regular basis.

Once my husband was introduced to the actual statistics of emergencies (which is low for a healthy low-risk woman), and he balanced that with the hospital being just across the street, I wouldn't say he was sold, but at least he no longer had any arguments.

The third item I wanted to sell my husband on was the toughest sell. He just could not picture me going through delivery without pain medication. My husband knows me too well. When it comes to pain, I am a wimp. My eyes still fill up with tears every time I get a shot.

I had him read books about the natural childbirth methods I had chosen. He saw me regularly practicing my relaxation techniques. He also saw the commitment and strong belief I had in myself. Eventually, I had to tell him that if he didn't believe I could do it, he would need to fake it, since during delivery it was his duty to be my main positive coach. From then on he never questioned (at least out loud) whether I could do it without pain medication.

In the end, I did make it through labor without medications. It was the most amazing experience of both of our lives. Looking back, neither of us would have done anything differently. The best way I can describe it is like playing not just one, but two exhausting sporting events in a row, and winning the championship in the end. Childbirth is a very powerful and fulfilling event.

Keep in mind that my natural childbirth experience was fulfilling because it met my needs and my desires. I have many friends who have had amazing birth experiences while using pain medications in hospitals. Those experiences met their needs and their desires. Then there are individuals who didn't find their experience amazing at all. In the end, any event that leads to a healthy child and mother (whether natural, medicated, or C section) is truly a great event.

# CHAPTER 14

# Breast-Feeding

## Breast-Feeding Considerations

Breast-feeding is a very personal decision. Do your research, consider all the factors, evaluate your situation, and weigh your options before making up your mind.

Today, there are numerous benefits and a few drawbacks to breast-feeding. The number one benefit is that breast milk has been found by numerous medical studies to be the best source of sustenance for most children. Due to these studies, women who choose not to breast-feed (or stop early) are often made to feel guilty about their decision. Do not let the opinions of others influence you. If you decide to forgo breast-feeding, keep in mind that there are many healthy women between the ages of twenty and forty who were raised on formula. In addition, today's formulas are far better than those found a few decades ago.

On the other hand, if you decide to breast-feed and continue working, there are a few obstacles that you will have to learn to overcome. The foremost of these is the lack of time. Feeding a baby formula is very simple. It can take less than a minute to prepare. Just add water to the powder mixture and you are ready to feed. A mother's effort is not required for this feat. Fathers and caregivers can easily take over this responsibility. However, breast-feeding squarely rests on a mother's shoulders. It's not something that can easily be passed off. There are several reasons that breast-feeding is much more time-consuming than formula feeding:

- Formula is not as easily digested by a baby as breast milk. Formula lasts in the baby's stomach much longer, and therefore, the baby does not need to be fed as often. By contrast, it's not unusual for a newborn to be up every two hours breast-feeding. It's tough to keep up this schedule when you have work the next morning.

  When I found myself extremely sleep-deprived, I would pump extra during the day, just so my husband could take over the late night feedings. Of course, this meant that I had to find the extra time during the day to pump.

- It takes longer for a baby to breast-feed than to bottle-feed. On the other hand, the advantage to breast-fed babies is that they have better tooth and jaw development because of breast-feeding.

- Working mothers who must leave their children with caregivers have to supply pumped breast milk. Pumping is very time-consuming. A baby can often drink breast milk faster than a pump can pump it. Depending upon the pump and the mother's breasts, pumping can take between ten minutes and a half hour to complete. If you plan on being away nine hours during a single day, at a minimum, you should pump twice. However, most women find that in order to keep up their milk supply they need to pump between three to five times a day at work. I had to turn down many invitations to lunch in order to pump. Not pumping as much as necessary increases the chance of getting a breast infection.

## A FEW OF THE BENEFITS OF BREAST-FEEDING

There have been many studies that have attributed medical benefits to breast-feeding. This section includes a few of the known benefits.

Studies indicate that there is no formula that can currently match that of breast milk. A mother's milk can change from one feeding to another to try to match her baby's nutritional needs. For example, a mother can produce antibodies for a germ that a baby has come in contact with. The mother then passes those antibodies to her baby through her breast milk, reducing her child's chance of getting sick. There aren't any formulas that can do this.

Studies comparing breast-fed and formula-fed babies report a reduced rate of infection, colds, and viruses among those that were breast-fed. Other studies report reduced incidence of illnesses such as diabetes. Breast-fed babies are less likely to develop allergies than their formula-fed counterparts. Babies that have been breast-fed also have a reduced chance of sudden infant death syndrome (SIDS).

There are also numerous benefits to mothers that breast-feed. These benefits begin immediately after the baby is born. The initial sucking by the baby at the breast triggers uterine contractions that reduces the mother's bleeding.

The production of breast milk eats up a lot of calories and makes it easier for many mothers to lose the weight accumulated during pregnancy. A special bonding takes place between a mother and a breast-fed baby. Breast-feeding forces busy women to take the time to slow down and focus on what's important. While breast-feeding, women release a hormone that is naturally calming. Breast-feeding reduces a woman's chance of developing breast cancer. Breast-feeding is less expensive than purchasing formula.

## Balancing Breast-Feeding with Work

There are several obstacles related to balancing breast-feeding and work, many of which involve pumping. Even though very few people know what pumping is, the majority of women who breast-feed and work pump. Pumping is the process of obtaining extra milk so that the baby can continue to drink breast milk rather than formula when the mother is not available to breast-feed.

The notion of being hooked up to a piece of equipment to express milk is a little strange at first. If you mention pumping milk, most people will picture a large machine hooked up to a cow rather than a small one attached to a woman. However, it is extremely common today. It's just not often discussed outside close friends who are breast-feeding or who have breast-fed in the past.

Once you have mastered breast-feeding and the soreness (pain in some instances) is gone, most women do not experience any pain when using good electric pumps. However, cheap pumps and non-electric pumps can cause problems. Speak with your lactation consultant about what pump to buy. Test your pump slowly. If it does not feel right, call your lactation consultant.

There are several good pumps on the market. The one I went with was Medela's Pump in Style. At $250, it's more expensive than most; however, my personal and professional needs mandated it. Women in other professions or those who do not travel may not need the extras that come with this pump. When deciding on a pump, base your decision on your own set of circumstances and needs. Here are the main reasons I chose the Pump in Style:

1. Nobody knows it's a breast pump. It is self-contained in a black case that looks like a briefcase or a computer case. Because I travel and must maintain a certain appearance, it's important that the pump I carry into any office, plant, or courthouse provides the same professional impression that my purse and briefcase do. I needed a pump that would not detract from my appearance. A bright pink pump would not have worked for me.

2. The case has an interior insulated compartment that can hold a blue ice pack and expressed milk. Carrying a small cooler would have worked just as well for storing pumped milk, but again no one knew I was carrying a cooler with this pump.

3. The pump includes adapters for both regular electrical outlets and vehicle lighter outlets. When traveling, I have found that the best place to pump is in rental cars. It's often cleaner and more private than airplanes, airports, and public rest rooms.

## SUPPLY & DEMAND

Mother Nature is truly amazing. When a baby is about to go through a growth spurt and will soon need extra nutrition, the baby instinctively starts sucking at the breast more. Babies often double the time they spend sucking just prior to these growth spurts. This extra sucking instructs the mother's breast to automatically start producing more milk in the near future. The opposite is true when the baby begins to suck less. During those periods, a mother will soon be producing less milk.

Pumping takes advantage of this milk production scheduling. Assume a mother has plans to go out to dinner with friends on Friday night. Her husband will be staying home with the baby. If the mother has stored extra pumped milk in the refrigerator, she'll have fewer concerns. But creating that extra supply will take planning.

If a mother pumps one bottle just before she leaves for the evening, it will probably not be enough to satisfy the baby if she is gone for several hours. Several days before the scheduled outing, the mother should begin increasing her production of milk by dry pumping. Dry pumping is the process of continuing to pump after the breasts have been emptied of milk (either by the baby or the pump). After doing this a few times, you should have a better estimate of how long you need to dry pump and how many days before the event you need to do this in order to produce the extra milk that you will need.

Breast milk stores very well when taken care of properly. Here are the general rules for milk storage:

- Milk placed immediately in a refrigerator (32 to 39°F) is good for up to 5 days.
- Milk placed immediately in a freezer section of a regular refrigerator freezer (not a freezer section located within the refrigerator compartment) is good for up to 3 months.
- Thawed milk is good in the refrigerator for up to 24 hours.

Always verify that the milk has not spoiled before feeding it to the baby. Spoiled milk smells sour and tastes bad.

It's important to ensure that there is more milk left with the caregiver than you estimate the baby will eat during your absence. Babies often surprise you by consuming more milk than expected.

If you have a longer trip scheduled or you plan on going back to work in the near future, it's best to start increasing your production and saving milk early.

## PUMPING AT WORK

Unlike breast-feeding, which can be accomplished discreetly, there is no way to inconspicuously and tactfully pump in front of others. Therefore, the biggest obstacle to overcome at work is to locate a private room with an electrical outlet that is available on a regular basis.

When working from a home office, it's much easier to manage pumping. On most of the days when I worked out of my home office, my daughter was downstairs while I worked upstairs. Since she could empty the milk much quicker than the pump, it was an easy choice: I'd much rather spend the quality time with her, than hooked up to the pump. However, since most women do not work out of their homes (or only occasionally do), pumping at a work location is often a necessity. The best scenario is when an employer has dedicated a special room just for that purpose. Of course, very few companies provide such comforts. Of the few that do, almost all have a large number of young female employees.

For those women with private offices, the question of where to pump is eliminated. However, other obstacles still remain. The main obstacle is that most offices do not have locks on their doors. Everyone knows at least one coworker who will peak his head in the door without knocking to see if you are on the phone or in a meeting. Being caught in the act of pumping creates a very uncomfortable situation. When I am in the corporate office, I have found that having a lookout (generally the person sitting just outside the door) works fairly well. The lookout will need to be told that if anyone comes to see you, they are not to enter while the door is closed.

For the many women who do not have private offices, the next best strategy is to borrow an office that is currently empty. However with office space often being limited, finding an unoccupied office may be an impossible task. Many women resort to borrowing someone else's office. If you decide to do this, make sure the length and frequency of your pumping sessions do not place an undue burden on the person lending you the office. Other women find that heading out to their cars provides them with a private clean location to accomplish pumping.

The alternate locations left for the women who do not have offices available to them and who cannot head out to their cars tend to be less appealing. That said, many women adjust and make use of these alternatives everyday. It's not unusual for mothers to be found pumping in storage closets, electrical closets, rest rooms, and lounges. These are not necessarily the most sanitary and discreet places, but they get the job done. Depending upon your circumstances, you may have to use your creativity to locate a place that will fit your needs.

Just when you think you have eliminated all obstacles, something is going to happen. Almost every woman who pumps at work has a story. I thought I had everything covered. Pumping in a private office on the thirtieth floor, a lookout in the hall, and my back turned towards the door. What could possibly happen? Then I looked up to see the window washer outside less than two feet from me. From his look, he definitely thought I was into some type of S&M. He then disappeared down the side of the building with a new story to tell his buddies.

## PUMPING & TRAVELING

When traveling and pumping, it is necessary to have a pumping schedule. Determine the times that you would like to pump (best-case scenario) and compare that with your itinerary. If you are in meetings or otherwise unavailable at these times, you will need to bump your pumping schedule up or push it back.

Again, the best locations are private, clean, and with an electrical outlet. Airplanes, airports, and private rest rooms should only be used as a last resort. Whenever I had to use one of these unsanitary locations, I always dumped the milk. I never wanted to take the chance of feeding my daughter contaminated milk. Pumping and dumping is very tough for mothers. Building up a good supply of excess milk for caregivers is very difficult and time-consuming. Mothers often treat pumped milk like gold, never wanting to waste a drop.

When I am traveling on business, I often have to visit unfamiliar offices, plants, and courthouses. Rental cars and hotels are often the best places to pump during such trips. When planning your trip, compare the cost of renting a car with the cost of taking a taxi. A one-day car rental may be comparable, and it will provide you with a pumping solution.

When locating a place to park for pumping, I always attempt to look for an area free from other cars and pedestrian traffic. But no matter how remote the location seems to be, I always find myself wondering if someone watching a security camera is having a good laugh at my expense.

A good friend of mine once had to park in a full parking lot in order to pump. Because the back windows were tinted, she jumped in the back seat for a little more privacy. It was hot that day, so she left the car running with the air conditioning on and locked the doors. Someone thinking that the car was mistakenly left running pressed up against the window for a better look. My friend is unsure how much of an eyeful that passerby caught.

When saving expressed milk overnight, make sure your hotel has a mini-bar or an in-room refrigerator. I have found that the coldest temperatures reached by many hotel mini-bars and refrigerators is often above 39°F. I never wanted to risk the milk going bad, so I always put it in the freezer section.

When preparing to leave for a trip, leave plenty of expressed milk with the caregiver. If there is not enough milk saved to cover the entire length of the trip, you may need to overnight some of the milk expressed while traveling. I had to do this on a handful of occasions when unplanned trips popped up. On one such occasion, I had three days of stored milk in the refrigerator, and I was going to be gone for five days (three nights). I managed by placing a frozen blue pack and the frozen expressed milk pumped during the first two days of the trip into a small soft-sided cooler. I placed the cooler inside an overnight express pack. It arrived at home the next morning, just as it began to thaw. The rest of the milk that I pumped during the trip was brought home with me on the plane. Of course, packing the cooler, the extra blue frozen pack, and the express mailing pack took some planning before I left for the trip.

### Breast Infections

The longer the trip, the more likely the amount of milk that you are producing will decrease. During a long trip, it's also more likely that you will suffer from a breast infection (clogged milk duct). Therefore, it's very important to make trips as short as possible. Always book the earliest flights that you can. The earliest flights are less likely to be delayed or cancelled. If a cancellation does occur, the earlier you start out, the more likely you will be able to catch another flight.

The best way to avoid these infections is not to skip or reduce how often you are pumping while you are away. Many women are enticed to postpone or skip pumping sessions when they have a full work schedule and they have peace of mind that they have left plenty of milk at home. Do not pump less when traveling.

Breast infections are often indicated by a hot red lump and flu symptoms followed by a high fever. Once you have an idea that you may be getting an infection, call your doctor or midwife. You may be able to avoid antibiotics by taking a hot shower and doing extra pumping on the infected side. When traveling, keep in mind that most hospitals with maternity wards have a lactation consultant available to answer questions over the phone or to see you in person.

## Airport Nuisances

The security stations at airports provide an added nuisance for pumping mothers. Their X-ray machines often detect the pumps as an electronic device. Seldom do these security personnel know what the machine is. The parts of my machine are sewn internally so they cannot get to them. This baffles them even further. One security guard to whom I had to explain what the pump was, started tearing the pump bag apart. I asked him not to handle the bags of milk for fear of contamination. He did it anyway and touched every bag with his dirty fingers. What an idiot and what a waste of good milk.

When traveling abroad, be sure to take your pump instructions with you. I have heard stories about experiences with security officials from several women who travel to less-developed countries. Often, those officials do not believe a woman's explanation of what a breast pump does. The instructions may help to get the point across.

Now that airlines have limited passengers to two pieces of carry-on luggage, when you are boarding a plane you may again be forced to tell airport personnel what your pump is for. In my eyes, pumps fall under of the category of a medical necessity. Medical necessities do not count towards the two-item limit for carry-ons. If anyone attempts to question you when you are carrying three bags and one is your pump, the statement "This is a breast pump and is considered a medical necessity" generally ends the pressure placed on you to check one of your bags.

Of course, there are always exceptions. I ran into one obsessive stewardess who told me breast pumps were not on her approved list of medical devices, and that I would have to check it. I explained that the airline provided her with a list of examples, not with a list of the "only" acceptable devices. She still wasn't buying it. I further explained that if I was forced to stay inside the plane for hours (which has happened to me on more than one occasion), I would become engorged and probably get an infection (which for me does automatically occur). Therefore, my pump is an absolute medical necessity. Imagine being stuck in a plane on the ground for hours, with little circulation, no food, no pump, and your breasts becoming painfully engorged. She let it go when a more reasonable stewardess told her that she thought the pump would meet the definition of a medical necessity.

Three carry-ons may sound like over-packing, but it's not. When I make a day trip in and out of a location, I often need my computer, my briefcase, and my pump — all of which I use throughout the day. I cannot afford the airline losing any of them. The only way to ensure that they arrive with me is to place them onboard myself. I have had past experiences with airlines losing my luggage. Keep in mind that if anything does happen to your pump while traveling, many hospitals rent them and many baby stores sell them.

Of course, who has time to do those things when you have a full day planned.

When unusual situations arise, you may need to rely on the kindness of strangers to get you through. One trip was supposed to take me a total of seven hours to arrive at my final destination. In the middle, there was supposed to be a two-hour layover at an airport I knew well. It had a room where I had pumped in the past. However, this flight turned into a twenty-two-hour ordeal at another airport that did not have anyplace for me to pump (not even an outlet in the bathroom). The airport was filled with angry people, and all the hotels were full. Had the airline told us the truth and not kept saying that it would only be another hour before we took off, I would have rented a car in order to have had a place to pump (and possibly sleep). After speaking with several individuals from the airport and airline, I finally found a Delta manager (my angel) who lent me her office so I could pump. I will always remember that day and her kindness.

## How Long To Breast-Feed

Many women wonder how long they should breast-feed. Medical research shows the longer, the better. However, the research also shows that any time spent breast-feeding is better for the child than no time at all. Even breast-feeding a few days is supposed to be beneficial.

Although everything I read said breast-feeding is not painful when done correctly, I found it initially very painful. For the first three weeks of nursing, I had pain during the first three minutes of each feeding. After the first three minutes were over, I became numb and the pain would disappear. After three weeks of nursing, there was no more pain.

I initially hoped to nurse for three months. Instead, I nursed for the first year (exclusively for the first six months until solids were added to her diet). I was able to nurse longer than originally anticipated because

- my daughter's desire to nurse was so strong,
- it provided a special bond between us (especially when I would finish working for the day or when I would come home from a trip), and
- everything I read pointed to the fact that it was the best thing I could do for her.

I have friends who didn't breast-feed and friends who breast-fed for the first two years. All of our circumstances were very different. Do what's best for you and your children without worrying what others think.

For more information on breast-feeding, a good place to start is with La Leche League's Web site (www.lalecheleague.org).

# Closing

Everyone has different goals, resources, and life experiences. When making your decisions, do what's best for you. You know better than anyone else what's right for you.

Find employers who meet your needs and make you happy. Do not try to fit into an atmosphere that does not fit your personality. Square pegs are unhappy trying to fit into round holes. Find employers who fit the shape of your peg.

When the study participants were asked what they would change if they had it all to do over again, only 32% would not change a thing. Overwhelmingly, participants wanted to either change their majors, the companies they worked for, the positions they went for, or their occupations.

For example, 7% of the study participants came out on their own and said they would have become doctors.

Several of the desired changes could have originally been avoided by performing more research and analysis before the original decisions were made. However, not all of the changes that they would have made in hindsight could have been predicted with additional research and analysis. Individuals change over time due to their experiences. Positive experiences increase our self–esteem and our belief in what we can do. The problem is that fears hold us back because of an uncertainty in our capabilities. When the study participants were asked what specifically they would want to convey to you, the number one item was that *you can be anything and do anything you put your mind to. Don't let fear hold you back.*

Do something you really love. If you find that you are unhappy, look into making a change. Several of the women that I interviewed went back to school in order to enter a different profession. Other women changed directions in their careers midstream. I interviewed a nurse who went into sales, a lawyer who became an accountant, an advertising specialist who went back to school and became a lawyer, and a business professional who went back to school and became a teacher.

But at the end of the day, recognize the fact that your career is only one part of your life. Your family, friends, and outside interests should be given just as much attention. Take time to enjoy the world. It's a wonderful place if you get the chance to stop and enjoy it.

*****

I am interested in hearing your feedback, anecdotes, and related examples that could be used to enhance future editions of this book. Please send your comments to jskarbek@home.com.

Good luck with your future endeavors.

— *Janet Skarbek*

# The Study Participants' Demographics

- 16% of the participants were homemakers.
- 25% worked part-time (less than forty hours a week).
- 43% worked forty to fifty hours per week.
- 16% worked more than fifty hours per week.

<br>

- 22% single
- 76% married
- 1% divorced
- 1% divorced and remarried.

<br>

- 5% did not expect children to be part of their future.
- 59% had children.
- 36% planned to have children at some future time.

The women who had children and/or expected to have children in the future had an average 1.25 children at the time of the study. They expected to have an additional 1.42 children during their lives, for an average 2.67 children expected.

Professions
- 16% homemakers
- 8% nurses
- 8% in finance/marketing
- 7% attorneys
- 6% teachers
- 5% accountants
- 5% engineers (environmental, civil, electrical, and process)
- 5% in sales
- 3% nurse practitioners
- 3% in computer science
- 2% entrepreneurs (owned businesses)

The rest of the participants were from various other fields, including social work, bank management, commercial property management, physical therapy, communications management, optometry, insurance, contract negotiations, mental health, and freelance writing.

47% of the participants had graduate degrees. Graduate fields included finance, engineering, marketing, nurse practitioning, math, graphic design, counseling, early childhood development, law, human resources, political science, social work, applied statistics, education, organic chemistry, dentistry, school psychology, and optometry.

The study participants (excluding homemakers) classified their professions as

- mostly female professions 33% of the time,
- mostly male professions 19% of the time, and
- co-ed professions 48% of the time.

A significant portion of the study participants resided in the northeastern United States (Maine to Maryland). However, a number of study participants lived outside that region. Study participants residing outside the Northeast came from California, Colorado, Florida, Illinois, Michigan, North Carolina, Ohio, Texas, Virginia, and Wisconsin.

Of the participants who worked, 27% "at times" work out of a home office. Of that 27%,

- 45% worked mostly out of their home office
- 9% worked half their week out of the home office
- 41% worked one day a week out of the home office, and
- 5% worked once a month out of the home office.

31% worked flexible hours (e.g., 8 a.m. to 4 p.m. on Mondays and noon to 8 p.m. on Tuesdays).

6% shared a job with another person.

42% had switched employers to increase their salaries/compensation.

40% had switched employers to get out of dead-end positions.

# Select Statements from the Equal Employment Opportunity Commission Regarding Discrimination

The mission of the Equal Employment Opportunity Commission (EEOC), as set forth in its strategic plan, is to promote equal opportunity in employment through administrative and judicial enforcement of the federal civil rights laws, and through education and technical assistance. Information included on the EEOC's home page includes annual reports, addresses, and phone numbers of field offices, press releases, fact sheets, and periodicals. The information contained in the rest of Appendix 2 came directly from several areas on their site http://www.eeoc.gov. Check this site for changes and updates.

## OVERVIEW OF EEOC ENFORCEMENT ACTIVITIES

The EEOC carries out its work at headquarters and in 50 field offices throughout the United States. Individuals who believe they have been discriminated against in employment begin our processes by filing administrative charges. Individual Commissioners may also initiate charges that the law has been violated. Through the investigation of charges, if the EEOC determines there is "reasonable cause" to believe that discrimination has occurred, it must then seek to conciliate the charge to reach a voluntary resolution between the charging party and the respondent. If conciliation is not successful, the EEOC may bring suit in federal court. Whenever the EEOC concludes its processing of a case, or earlier upon the request of a charging party, it issues a "notice of right to sue," which enables the charging party to bring an individual action in court.

The Commission also issues regulatory and other forms of guidance interpreting the laws it enforces, is responsible for the federal sector employment discrimination program, provides funding and support to state and local fair employment practices agencies (FEPAs), and conducts broad-based outreach and technical assistance programs.

## STATUTORY AUTHORITY

The U.S. Equal Employment Opportunity Commission was established by Title VII of the Civil Rights Act of 1964 and began operating on July 2, 1965. The EEOC enforces the principal federal statutes prohibiting employment discrimination, including:

- Title VII of the Civil Rights Act of 1964, as amended, which prohibits employment discrimination on the basis of race, color, religion, sex, or national origin;
- the Age Discrimination in Employment Act of 1967, as amended (ADEA), which prohibits employment discrimination against individuals 40 years of age or older;
- the Equal Pay Act of 1963 (EPA), which prohibits discrimination on the basis of gender in compensation for substantially similar work under similar conditions;
- the Title I of the Americans with Disabilities Act of 1990 (ADA), which prohibits employment discrimination on the basis of disability in both the public and private sector, excluding the federal government;
- the Civil Rights Act of 1991, which includes provisions for monetary damages in cases of intentional discrimination and clarifies provisions regarding disparate impact actions, and,
- Section 501 of the Rehabilitation Act of 1973, as amended which prohibits employment discrimination against federal employees with disabilities.

## *What Discriminatory Practices Are Prohibited by These Laws?*

Under Title VII, the ADA, and the ADEA, it is illegal to discriminate in any aspect of employment, including:

- hiring and firing;
- compensation, assignment, or classification of employees;
- transfer, promotion, layoff, or recall;
- job advertisements;
- recruitment;
- testing;
- use of company facilities;
- training and apprenticeship programs;
- fringe benefits;
- pay, retirement plans, and disability leave; or
- other terms and conditions of employment.

Discriminatory practices under these laws also include:

- harassment on the basis of race, color, religion, sex, national origin, disability, or age;
- retaliation against an individual for filing a charge of discrimination, participating in an investigation, or opposing discriminatory practices;
- employment decisions based on stereotypes or assumption about the abilities, traits, or performance of individuals of a certain sex, race, age, religion, or ethnic group, or individuals with disabilities;
- denying employment opportunities to a person because of marriage to, or association with, an individuals of a particular race, religion, national origin, or an individual with a disability. Title VII also prohibits discrimination because of participation in schools or places of worship associated with a particular racial, ethnic, or religious group.

## TITLE VII OF THE CIVIL RIGHTS ACT OF 1964

Title VII prohibits not only intentional discrimination, but also practices that have the effect of discriminating against individuals because of their race, color, national origin, religion, or sex.

Title VII's broad prohibition against sex discrimination specifically covers

- Sexual Harassment — This includes practices ranging from direct requests for sexual favors to workplace conditions that create a hostile environment for persons of either gender. (The "hostile environment" standard also applies to harassment on the bases of race, color, national origin, religion, age, and disability.)
- Pregnancy Based Discrimination — Pregnancy, childbirth, and related medical conditions must be treated in the same way as other temporary illnesses or conditions.

*Additional rights are available to parents and others under the Family and Medical Leave Act (FMLA), which is enforced by the U.S. Department of Labor. For information on the FMLA, or to file an FMLA complaint, individuals should contact the nearest office of the Wage and Hour Division, Employment Standards Administration, U.S. Department of Labor. The Wage and Hour Division is listed in most telephone directories under U.S. Government, Department of Labor.*

## FACTS ABOUT SEXUAL HARASSMENT

Sexual harassment is a form of sex discrimination that violates Title VII of the Civil Rights Act of 1964.

Unwelcome sexual advances, requests for sexual favors, and other verbal or physical conduct of a sexual nature constitutes sexual harassment when submission to or rejection of this conduct explicitly or implicitly affects an individual's employment, unreasonably interferes with an individual's work performance or creates an intimidating, hostile or offensive work environment.

Sexual harassment can occur in a variety of circumstances, including but not limited to the following:

- The victim as well as the harasser may be a woman or a man. The victim does not have to be of the opposite sex.
- The harasser can be the victim's supervisor, an agent of the employer, a supervisor in another area, a co-worker, or a non-employee.
- The victim does not have to be the person harassed but could be anyone affected by the offensive conduct.
- Unlawful sexual harassment may occur without economic injury to or discharge of the victim.
- The harasser's conduct must be unwelcome.

It is helpful for the victim to directly inform the harasser that the conduct is unwelcome and must stop. The victim should use any employer complaint mechanism or grievance system available.

When investigating allegations of sexual harassment, EEOC looks at the whole record: the circumstances, such as the nature of the sexual advances, and the context in which the alleged incidents occurred. A determination on the allegations is made from the facts on a case-by-case basis.

Prevention is the best tool to eliminate sexual harassment in the workplace. Employers are encouraged to take steps necessary to prevent sexual harassment from occurring. They should clearly communicate to employees that sexual harassment will not be tolerated. They can do so by establishing an effective complaint or grievance process and taking immediate and appropriate action when an employee complains.

## FACTS ABOUT PREGNANCY DISCRIMINATION

The Pregnancy Discrimination Act is an amendment to Title VII of the Civil Rights Act of 1964. Discrimination on the basis of pregnancy, childbirth or related medical conditions constitutes unlawful sex discrimination under Title VII. Women affected by pregnancy or related conditions must be treated in the same manner as other applicants or employees with similar abilities or limitations.

### 1. Hiring

An employer cannot refuse to hire a woman because of her pregnancy related condition as long as she is able to perform the major functions of her job. An employer cannot refuse to hire her because of its prejudices against pregnant workers or the prejudices of co-workers, clients or customers.

### 2. Pregnancy and Maternity Leave

An employer may not single out pregnancy related conditions for special procedures to determine an employee's ability to work. However, an employer may use any procedure used to screen other employees' ability to work. For example, if an employer requires its employees to submit a doctor's statement concerning their inability to work before granting leave or paying sick benefits, the employer may require employees affected by pregnancy related conditions to submit such statements.

If an employee is temporarily unable to perform her job due to pregnancy, the employer must treat her the same as any other temporarily disabled employee; for example, by providing modified tasks, alternative assignments, disability leave or leave without pay.

Pregnant employees must be permitted to work as along as they are able to perform their jobs. If an employee has been absent from work as a result of a pregnancy related condition and recovers, her employer may not require her to remain on leave until the baby's birth. An employer may not have a rule which prohibits an employee from returning to work for a predetermined length of time after childbirth.

Employers must hold open a job for a pregnancy related absence the same length of time jobs are held open for employees on sick or disability leave.

*3. Health Insurance*

Any health insurance provided by an employer must cover expenses for pregnancy related conditions on the same basis as costs for other medical conditions. Health insurance for expenses arising from abortion is not required, except where the life of the mother is endangered.

Pregnancy related expenses should be reimbursed exactly as those incurred for other medical conditions, whether payment is on a fixed basis or a percentage of reasonable and customary charge basis.

The amounts payable by the insurance provider can be limited only to the same extent as costs for other conditions. No additional, increased or larger deductible can be imposed.

If a health insurance plan excludes benefit payments for pre-existing conditions when the insured's coverage becomes effective, benefits can be denied for medical costs arising from an existing pregnancy.

Employers must provide the same level of health benefits for spouses of male employees as they do for spouses of female employees.

*4. Fringe Benefits*

Pregnancy related benefits cannot be limited to married employees. In an all-female workforce or job classification, benefits must be provided for pregnancy related conditions if benefits are provided for other medical conditions.

If an employer provides any benefits to workers on leave, the employer must provide the same benefits for those on leave for pregnancy related conditions.

Employees with pregnancy related disabilities must be treated the same as other temporarily disabled employees for accrual and crediting of seniority, vacation calculation, pay increases and temporary disability benefits.

## EQUAL PAY ACT (EPA)

The EPA prohibits discrimination on the basis of sex in the payment of wages or benefits, where men and women perform work of similar skill, effort, and responsibility for the same employer under similar working conditions.

Note that:

- Employers may not reduce wages of either sex to equalize pay between men and women. Instead, the pay of the lower paid employee(s) must be increased.
- A violation of the EPA may occur where a different wage was/is paid to a person who worked in the same job before or after an employee of the opposite sex.
- A violation may also occur where a labor union causes the employer to violate the law.

The Equal Pay Act requires that men and women be given equal pay for equal work in the same establishment. The jobs need not be identical, but they must be substantially equal. It is job content, not job titles, that determines whether jobs are substantially equal.

Pay differentials are permitted when they are based on seniority, merit, quantity or quality of production, or a factor other than sex. These are known as "affirmative defenses" and it is the employer's burden to prove they apply.

## TITLE VII, ADEA, AND ADA

Title VII, the ADEA, and the ADA prohibit compensation discrimination on the basis of race, color, religion, sex, national origin, or disability. Unlike the EPA, there is no requirement under Title VII, the ADEA, or the ADA that the claimant's job be substantially equal to that of a higher paid person outside the claimant's protected class, nor do these statutes require the claimant to work in the same establishment as a comparator. The basic theories of disparate treatment and adverse impact generally apply to compensation discrimination claims under these statutes.

Compensation discrimination under Title VII, the ADEA, or the ADA can occur in a variety of forms. For example:

- An employer pays an employee with a disability less than similarly situated employees without disabilities and the employer's explanation (if any) does not satisfactorily account for the differential.
- A discriminatory compensation system has been discontinued but still has lingering discriminatory effects on present salaries. For example, if an employer has a compensation policy or practice that pays Hispanics lower salaries than other employees, the employer must not only adopt a new non-discriminatory compensation policy, it also must affirmatively eradicated salary disparities that began prior to the adoption of the new policy and make the victims whole.
- An employer sets the compensation for jobs predominately held by, for example, women or African-Americans below that suggested by the employer's job evaluation study, while the pay for jobs predominately held by men or whites is consistent with the level suggested by the job evaluation study.
- An employer maintains a neutral compensation policy or practice that has an adverse impact on employees in a protected class and cannot be justified as job-related and consistent with business necessity. For example, if an employer provides extra compensation to employees who are the "head of household," i.e., married with dependents and the primary financial contributor to the household, the practice may have an unlawful disparate impact on women.

Employers are encouraged to evaluate their compensation systems to ensure that the compensation of employees is based on nondiscriminatory factors. Employers also should evaluate practices that may indirectly depress the compensation of employees in protected classes. For example, employers should make sure that promotion decisions, performance appraisal systems, and procedures for assigning work are non-discriminatory.

### WHEN IS AN EMPLOYER LEGALLY RESPONSIBLE FOR HARASSMENT BY A SUPERVISOR?

An employer is always responsible for harassment by a supervisor that culminated in a tangible employment action. If the harassment did not lead to a tangible employment action, the employer is liable unless it proves that: 1) it exercised reasonable care to prevent and promptly correct any harassment; and 2) the employee unreasonably failed to complain to management or to avoid harm otherwise.

### DOES AN EMPLOYEE WHO IS HARASSED BY HIS OR HER SUPERVISOR HAVE ANY RESPONSIBILITIES?

Yes. The employee must take reasonable steps to avoid harm from the harassment. Usually, the employee will exercise this responsibility by using the employer's complaint procedure.

### IS AN EMPLOYER LEGALLY RESPONSIBLE FOR ITS SUPERVISOR'S HARASSMENT IF THE EMPLOYEE FAILED TO USE THE EMPLOYER'S COMPLAINT PROCEDURE?

No, unless the harassment resulted in a tangible employment action or unless it was reasonable for the employee not to complain to management. An employee's failure to complain would be reasonable, for example, if he or she had a legitimate fear of retaliation. The employer must prove that the employee acted unreasonably.

### WHICH EMPLOYERS AND OTHER ENTITIES ARE COVERED BY THESE LAWS?

Title VII and the ADA cover all private employers, state and local governments, and education institutions that employ 15 or more individuals. These laws also cover private and public employment agencies, labor organization, and joint labor management committees controlling apprenticeship and training.

The ADEA covers all private employers with twenty or more employees, state and local governments (including school districts), employment agencies and labor organizations.

The EPA covers all employees who are covered by the Federal Wage and Hour Law (the Fair Labor Standards Act). Virtually all employers are subject to the provisions of this Act.

Title VII, the ADEA, and the EPA also cover the federal government. In addition, the federal government is covered by Section 501 of the Rehabilitation Act of 1973, as amended, which incorporates the requirements of the ADA. However, different procedures are used for processing complaints for federal discrimination, contact the EEOC office of the federal agency where the alleged discrimination occurred.

## WHO CAN FILE A CHARGE OF DISCRIMINATION?

- Any individual who believes that his or her employment rights have been violated may file a charge of discrimination with the EEOC.
- In addition, an individual, organization, or agency may file a charge on behalf of another person in order to protect the aggrieved person's identity.

## HOW IS A CHARGE OF DISCRIMINATION FILED?

- A charge may be filed by mail or in person at the nearest EEOC office. Individuals may consult their local telephone directory (U.S. Government listing) or call 1-800-669-4000 (voice) or 1-800-669-6820 (TTY) to contact the nearest EEOC office for more information on specific procedures for filing a charge.
- Individuals who need an accommodation in order to file a charge (e.g., sign language interpreter, print materials in an accessible format) should inform the EEOC field office so appropriate arrangements can be made.

## WHAT INFORMATION MUST BE PROVIDED TO FILE A CHARGE?

- The complaining party's name, address, and telephone number;

- The name, address, and telephone number of the respondent employer, employment agency, or union that is alleged to have discrimination, and number of employees (union members), if known;
- A short description of the alleged violation (the event that caused the complaining party to believe that his or her rights were violated); and
- The date(s) of the alleged violation(s).

## What Are the Time Limits for Filing a Charge of Discrimination?

All laws enforced by EEOC, except the Equal Pay Act, require filing a charge with EEOC before a private lawsuit may be filed in court. There are strict time limits within which charges must be filed:

- A charge must be filed with EEOC within 180 days from the date of the alleged violation, in order to protect the charging party's rights.
- This 180-day filing deadline is extended to 300 days if the charge is also covered by a state or local anti-discrimination law. For ADEA charges, only state laws extend the filing limit to 300 days.
- These time limits do not apply to claims under the Equal Pay Act, because under that Act persons do not have to first file a charge with EEOC in order to have the right to go to court. However, since many EPA claims also raise Title VII sex discrimination issues, it may be advisable to file charges under both laws within the time limits indicated.
- To protect legal rights, it is always best to contact EEOC promptly when discrimination is suspected.

## What Agency Handles a Charge That Is Also Covered by State or Local Law?

Many states and localities have anti-discrimination laws and agencies responsible for enforcing those laws. The EEOC refers to these agencies as "Fair Employment Practices Agencies (FEPAs)." Through the use of "work sharing agreements," the EEOC and the FEPAs avoid duplication of effort while at the same time ensuring that a charging party's rights are protected under both federal and state law.

- If a charge is filed with a FEPA and is also covered by federal law, the FEPA "dual files" the charge with EEOC to protect federal rights. The charge usually will be retained by the FEPA for handling.
- If a charge is filed with the EEOC and also is covered by state or local law, the EEOC "dual files" the charge with the state or local FEPA, but ordinarily retains the charge for handling.

## WHAT HAPPENS AFTER A CHARGE IS FILED WITH THE EEOC?

The employer is notified that the charge has been filed. From this point there are a number of ways a charge may be handled:

- A charge may be assigned for priority investigation if the initial facts appear to support a violation of law. When the evidence is less strong, the charge may be assigned for follow-up investigation to determine whether it is likely that a violation has occurred.
  - EEOC can seek to settle a charge at any stage of the investigation if the charging party and the employer express an interest in doing so. If settlement efforts are not successful, the investigation continues.
  - In investigating a charge, EEOC may make written requests for information, interview people, review documents, and, as needed, visit the facility where the alleged discrimination occurred. When the investigation is complete, EEOC will discuss the evidence with the charging party or employer, as appropriate.

- The charge may be selected for EEOC's mediation program if both the charging party and the employer express an interest in this option. Mediation is offered as an alternative to a lengthy investigation. Participation in the mediation program is confidential, voluntary, and requires consent from both charging party and employer. If mediation is unsuccessful, the charge is returned for investigation.

- A charge may be dismissed at any point if, in the agency's best judgment, further investigation will not establish a violation of the law. A charge may be dismissed at the time it is filed, if an initial in-depth interview does not produce evidence to support the claim. When a charge is dismissed, a notice is issued in accordance with the law which gives the charging party 90 days in which to file a lawsuit on his or her own behalf.

## How Does EEOC Resolve Discrimination Charges?

- If the evidence obtained in an investigation does not establish that discrimination occurred, this will be explained to the charging party. A required notice is then issued, closing the case and giving the charging party 90 days in which to file a lawsuit on his or her own behalf.

- If the evidence establishes that discrimination has occurred, the employer and the charging party will be informed of this in a letter of determination that explains the finding. EEOC will then attempt conciliation with the employer to develop a remedy for the discrimination.

- If the case is successfully conciliated, or if a case has earlier been successfully mediated or settled, neither EEOC nor the charging party may go to court unless the conciliation, mediation, or settlement agreement is not honored.

- If EEOC is unable to successfully conciliate the case, the agency will decide whether to bring suit in federal court. If EEOC decides not to sue, it will issue a notice of closing the case and giving the charging party 90 days in which to file a lawsuit on his or her own behalf. In Title VII and ADA cases against state or local governments, the Department of Justice takes these actions.

## WHEN CAN AN INDIVIDUAL FILE AN EMPLOYMENT DISCRIMINATION LAWSUIT IN COURT?

A charging party may file a lawsuit within 90 days after receiving a notice of a "right to sue" from EEOC, as stated above. Under Title VII and the ADA, a charging party also can request a notice of "right to sue" from EEOC 180 days after the charge was first filed with the Commission, and may then bring suit within 90 days after receiving this notice. Under the ADEA, a suit may be filed at any time 60 days after filing a charge with EEOC, but not later than 90 days after EEOC gives notice that it has completed action on the charge.

Under EPA, a lawsuit must be filed within two years (three years for willful violations) of the discrimination act, which in most cases is payment of a discriminatory lower wage.

## WHAT REMEDIES ARE AVAILABLE WHEN DISCRIMINATION IS FOUND?

The "relief" or remedies available for employment discrimination, whether caused by intentional acts or by practices that have a discriminatory effect, may include:

- back pay,
- hiring,
- promotion,
- reinstatement,
- front pay,
- reasonable accommodation, or
- other actions that will make an individual "whole" (in the condition s/he would have been but for the discrimination).

Remedies also may include payment of:

- attorney's fees,
- expert witness fees, and
- court costs.

Under most EEOC-enforced laws, compensatory and punitive damages also may be available where intentional discrimination is found. Damages may be available to compensate for actual monetary losses, for future monetary losses, and for mental anguish and inconvenience. Punitive damages also may be available if an employer acted with malice or reckless indifference. Punitive damages are not available against state or local governments.

In cases concerning reasonable accommodation under the ADA, compensatory or punitive damages may not be awarded to the charging party if an employer can demonstrate that "good faith" efforts were made to provide reasonable accommodation.

An employer may be required to post notices to all employees addressing the violations of a specific charge and advising them of their rights under the laws EEOC enforces and their right to be free from retaliation. Such notices must be accessible, as needed, to persons with visual or other disabilities that affect reading.

The employer also may be required to take corrective or preventive actions to cure the source of the identified discrimination and minimize the chance of its recurrence, as well as discontinue the specific discriminatory practices involved in the case.

# Index

# THE PROFESSIONAL WOMEN'S INSTITUTE
Providing Support for Professional Women

# To Order a Book or To Find Out More about Janet Skarbek's Seminars

Call 1-888-668-0840 toll free.
For book orders, have your credit card ready.

Fax the below order form to 856-786-1688.

Send the below order form to
The Professional Women's Institute, PO Box 2590,
Cinnaminson, NJ 08077. USA.

*Planning Your Future: A Guide for Professional Women*
by Janet Skarbek: $19.95 each                                    _____

*She Who Dares Wins*
by Eileen Gillibrand & Jenny Mosley: $13.00 each       _____

Total cost of books                                                       _____

New Jersey shipments add 6% sales tax                        _____

Shipping/Handling: $3 for the first book and
$1.50 for each additional book. Please call for
international shipping rates.                                          _____

Total due                                                                     _____

**Where To Send the Shipment**

Name: _____

Address: _____

City: _____ State: _____ Zip: _____

Telephone: _____

**Payment Method**          Visa      MasterCard      Check

Name as it appears on card: _____

Credit Card#: _____ Exp. Date: _____

Signature: _____ Date: _____

*When ordering more than 5 books, please call for the discount.*

# THE PROFESSIONAL WOMEN'S INSTITUTE
Providing Support for Professional Women

# To Order a Book or To Find Out More about Janet Skarbek's Seminars

**Call 1-888-668-0840 toll free.**
For book orders, have your credit card ready.

**Fax the below order form to 856-786-1688.**

**Send the below order form to
The Professional Women's Institute, PO Box 2590,
Cinnaminson, NJ 08077. USA.**

*Planning Your Future: A Guide for Professional Women*
by Janet Skarbek: $19.95 each                    _____

*She Who Dares Wins*
by Eileen Gillibrand & Jenny Mosley: $13.00 each   _____

Total cost of books                                _____

New Jersey shipments add 6% sales tax              _____

Shipping/Handling: $3 for the first book and
$1.50 for each additional book. Please call for
international shipping rates.                       _____

Total due                                          _____

**Where To Send the Shipment**

Name: _____

Address: _____

City: _____ State: _____ Zip: _____

Telephone: _____

**Payment Method**          Visa    MasterCard    Check

Name as it appears on card: _____

Credit Card#: _____ Exp. Date: _____

Signature: _____ Date: _____

**When ordering more than 5 books, please call for the discount.**